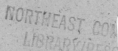 

745.593   41,268
C462w   Chapell, Carl
            Wildlife woodcarvers

NORTHEAST COMMUNITY COLLEGE
LIBRARY / RESOURCE CENTER
NORFOLK, NE   68701

WILDLIFE WOODCARVERS

WILDLIFE WOODCARVERS

A complete how-to-do-it book for carving and painting wildfowl

CARL CHAPELL
and
CLARK SULLIVAN

745.593
C462w

Stackpole Books

41,268

Copyright © 1986 by Stackpole Books

Published by
STACKPOLE BOOKS
Cameron and Kelker Streets
P.O. Box 1831
Harrisburg, PA 17105

All rights reserved, including the right to reproduce this book or
portions thereof in any form or by any means, electronic or mechanical,
including photocopying, recording, or by any information storage and
retrieval system, without permission in writing from the publisher.
All inquiries should be addressed to Stackpole Books, Cameron and
Kelker Streets, P.O. Box 1831, Harrisburg, Pennsylvania 17105.

Printed in the U.S.A.

Library of Congress Cataloging-in-Publication Data

Chapell, Carl.
    Wildlife woodcarvers.

    1. Decoys (Hunting) 2. Waterfowl in art. 3. Wood-
carving—Technique. 4. Painting—Technique.
I. Sullivan, Clark. II. Title.
NK9704.C44 1986   731.4′62   85–14874
ISBN 0-8117-1882-4

To Richard LeMaster

A gentleman and dedicated carver and author, whose books have taught and inspired countless numbers of novice carvers. Without his true dedication to this art, carving would not have grown to the fantastic art form we enjoy today. Thank you, Richard LeMaster. We miss you and your work.

Contents

Acknowledgments

If someone would have informed us of the magnitude of doing a book, we might have had second thoughts before we undertook such a venture.

But now that it is completed and we look back on all the trial and error, the sleepless nights, and all the other obstacles that we had to overcome, we realize that maybe it wasn't so bad after all.

We would like to take the time to thank some special people who helped us with this endeavor.

First of all, our photographer, Randy W. Carrels of Flint, Michigan, who took all the photographs in the book except the black and whites of the live ducks, and a few color shots that we took. Randy was always accessible and spent countless hours developing and re-shooting photographs that we somehow forgot. Without his dedication and expertise we would have had a much more diffi-

cult time. Thank you, Randy.

A special thank-you to our students who, through our classes, helped us to learn also.

Also, a thank-you to the thousands of viewers of "Wildlife Woodcarvers" throughout the United States and Canada, who wrote to inform us of their joy in carving; to John E. Heintz, Jr. of Marine City, Michigan, for his black and white photographs of the puddle and diving ducks; and to Frank Newmyer, "World Champion Taxidermist," whose splendid mounted creations are used in this book.

Last but not least, and most important we are told, are our wives, for putting up with our meetings, bad jokes, lapses of memory, and for not throwing away the mountains of photographs and papers we accumulated over five months of work. Thank you, Bobbi Sullivan and Bonnie Chapell.

Introduction

In five years of teaching carving classes, we have never had a student who could not do a good carving. It is true that some students do better than others because they have a good understanding of what wildfowl look like. Others have more desire and still others just plain try harder because they realize their lack of formal training.

We have had students who entered our classes with self-imposed restrictions, saying things like "I can't do that" or "I don't have the talent." To statements such as these, we respond by saying simply, you can carve a good bird if you think you can.

The key message is a positive attitude and belief in yourself. This will do more for you than any instructor. We know we have convinced many a nonbeliever. No carving is a bad carving in our eyes. You have to start sometime and grow with experience. Every carving results in a feeling of accomplishment and pride. Do your homework and do

not give up. You will be surprised with the results.

Many of the photographs in this book represent the work of our students, some the results of those who said "I can't do that" or "I don't have the talent." We take little credit for their improvement, which, without the students' change in attitude and perseverance, would never have happened.

Our goal in writing this book is to give you a basic outline for carving, using photographs and sketches to aid you in understanding our instruction. We will follow the same basic format of our Public Broadcast Service television program, "Wildlife Woodcarvers."

In our program, we stress the importance of research and how important that knowledge is before you start carving. There are many books being published today on waterfowl carving, and they are all good because they share the knowledge of many great carvers. We buy every book we can because we want to grow with this fantastic art form. We suggest you grab every bit of knowledge you can, whether it's by reading a book or attending a show or watching a video.

We also tell you there are as many ways to carve a duck as there are ways to cook a duck. What we teach is by no means the best or only way to carve. Feel free to experiment on your own. Use your creative ability and you will grow quickly and enjoy your hobby to the fullest. Remember, your next bird is always your best bird.

The growth in carving in the past ten years has been phenomenal, and we see no end in sight. We see new ideas by young and old carvers every year. We often wonder how much you can do to a carving to make it look better. Just when we think nothing more can possibly be done, somebody refines or invents a new technique.

If there is an aura about carving waterfowl, upland game birds, or song birds, it lies in the incredible realism attained by today's carvers. The beauty of the hobby is that special feeling of accomplishment and the burning desire to start the next carving.

1

Anatomy

Just the word *anatomy* may scare some novice carvers. You can relax because you do not have to be an ornithologist or game biologist in order to complete a carving. We do not suggest studying the skeletal structure of waterfowl and memorizing all the bones and muscles. We do, however, think it is important enough to do some research, so that you know what the structure of a given waterfowl looks like.

Waterfowl Categories

Before we take a look at anatomy, a brief lesson on waterfowl classification may be helpful. Three subfamilies of ducks are generally recognized: the *Fuligulinae*, or sea ducks; the *Anatidae*, or freshwater ducks; and the *Merginae*, or mergansers. These families are also defined as:

Dabbling ducks, or puddle ducks. These are the farm and river ducks (freshwater ducks). In order to fly they have to jump straight out of the water with the help of their long, powerful wings. These birds tip up, so to speak, when they feed. You can see their tails sticking up in the air as they dabble for food. Species in this category are: mallard, blue-winged teal, green-winged teal, cinnamon teal, shoveler (spoonbill), widgeon (baldpate), gadwall, wood duck, pintail, and black duck.

Diving ducks. These birds must run along the water in order to gain flight because of their short wings and heavy bodies. Their feet are situated far back on the body to aid diving and swimming underwater. Hunters have witnessed the ability of at least two species—bufflehead and ruddy duck—to come up from a dive and burst into flight right out

Dabbling duck, mallard.

Diving duck, lesser scaup.

of the water. Species in the divers' category are: bufflehead, canvasback, ringnecked duck, greater scaup, lesser scaup, redhead, old squaw, common goldeneye, barrows goldeneye, and ruddy duck.

Mergansers. These are the ducks commonly known as fish ducks. Species are: hooded mergansers, common mergansers, and redbreasted mergansers.

Interesting point—the word *duck* is the common name for the female of any species in the family *Anatidae.* The males are referred to as drakes and are more brilliantly colored. (In ordinary usage, both are referred to as ducks.) In general, though, *drake* refers to the male of the species and *hen,* the female.

Basic Terminology

Waterfowl anatomy has a vocabulary all its own. Study the drawings so that you understand and remember the various areas. Start using the terminology—mandible, primaries, scapular, and so on—they will be important in your research later on.

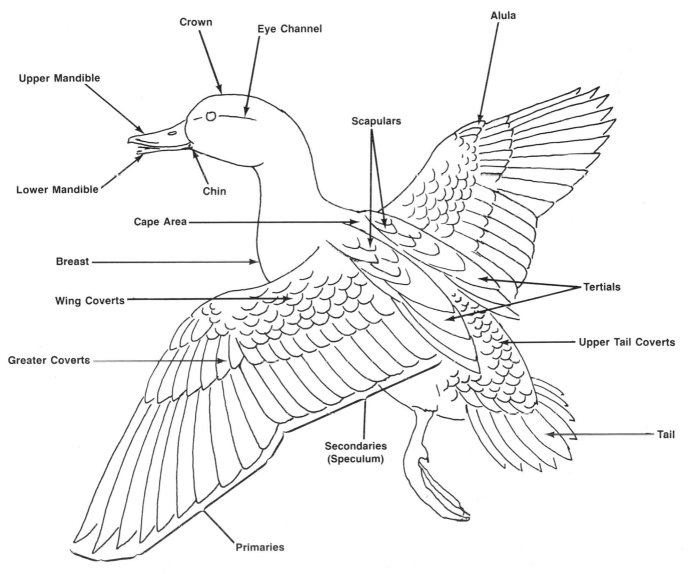

Waterfowl anatomy.

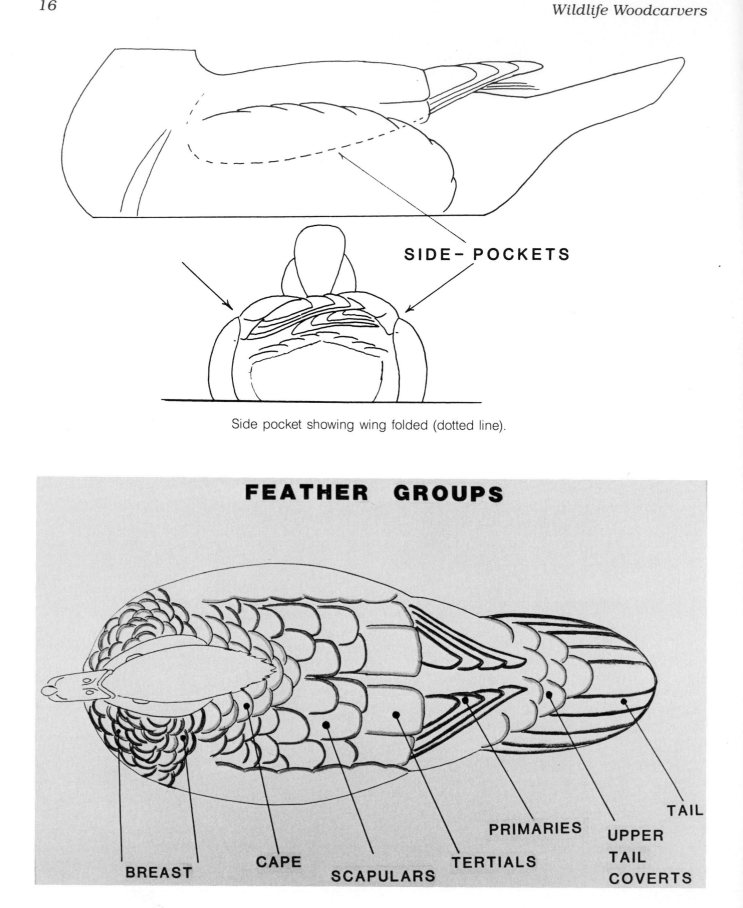

SIDE-POCKETS

Side pocket showing wing folded (dotted line).

FEATHER GROUPS

BREAST

CAPE

SCAPULARS

TERTIALS

PRIMARIES

UPPER TAIL COVERTS

TAIL

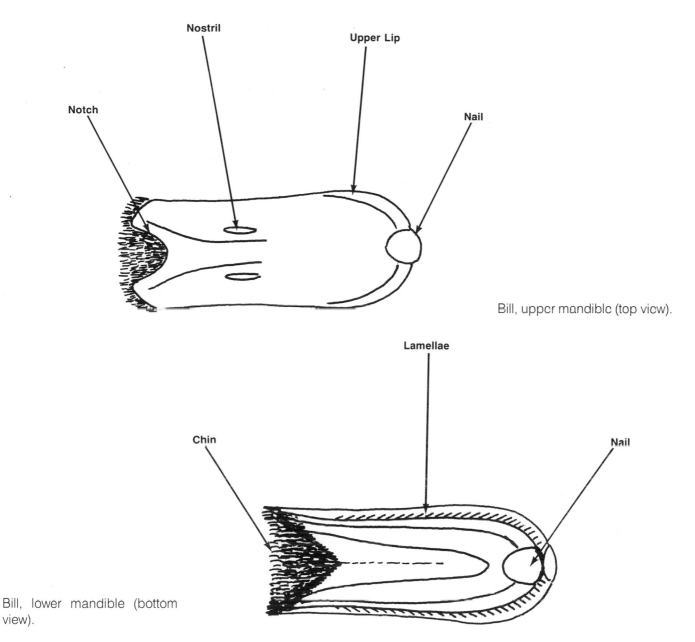

Bill, upper mandible (top view).

Bill, lower mandible (bottom view).

Motion and Muscle Definition

Carving a bird to represent some implied motion is possible once you know where the bones connect and what happens to the bird when he moves his head, leg, or wing. The motion does not stop there, however. A simple action, such as preening the side area, can involve a chain of muscle movements that extends throughout the entire body.

Carving the features and muscles accentuated by such a motion tends to give your piece character and life. (This is sometimes referred to as "cheesecaking." What we really do is over-carve some areas in order to animate the carving.)

It's important to train yourself to see movement in the correct perspective *before* you try to carve. One way to train yourself is to start with a photograph of a bird in a particular position and, beginning with the bill, write down everything you see from the nail on the end of the bill to where the nostrils are, bill separation, and so forth. Do this from the tip of the bill to the tail. Don't forget to write down such features as colors and feather shapes, position of the head, whether it is high or low. Go back a day later and do the same thing, but do not look at your notes. Surprised? We were. This process really aids you in seeing the bird. Compare your notes and then do the same thing with another picture of the same bird in a different position.

Walk before you run. Keep the carvings simple; no preeners or sleepers unless you know the bird. You will have to do a lot of research, even for a simple low head carving. When you feel ready to get into more complicated carvings, let her rip. We know you can do it!

Widgeon (baldpate) preening side area. Note tail is turned toward head.

Swimming duck showing head and tail turned to meet each other. Photograph such a top view to later make a good pattern for your carving.

Teal drinking water. Notice muscle definition in jowl area and position of head and neck. Also note this makes tertials and primaries stick up higher.

Alert pintail, eyes wide open, skinny neck. The whole bird seems flat and tense.

Beautiful hen canvasback with head back between shoulders, ready for a snooze. Look at wrinkles in neck and double chin.

Sleeper. Note tilt to breast and head and neck off-center (to allow vertebrae to move to sleeping position without breaking). Also note feather line of neck.

Rights and Wrongs of Anatomy

Now let's focus on some important areas where errors commonly occur. These errors can be avoided to a certain degree by remembering one word, *research*. We don't expect you to do a perfect carving because you are trying to duplicate life out of wood. We are still striving to learn ourselves. It seems that the "perfect carving" will remain an elusive goal, so we must adjust our understanding to a more lax version of the definition. Learn from each carving you do and go on to the next "perfect carving."

Looking at front of head, note that eyes are almost straight up and down. They sit in a socket area—called the eye channel—slightly angled so they look towards tip of bill. Note also roundness of top of head and jowl areas. It's possible for heads of some waterfowl to be flat or concave, so be careful.

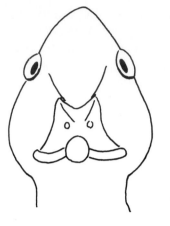

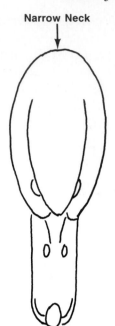

Narrow Neck

The cone head. Common error is to make top of head too pointed, which makes eyes look up to the clouds. The poor guy would really have difficulty making a landing on the water when his eyes are pointed up.

Correct top view of dabbling duck. Note how bill comes into head area straight and head starts flaring out to its widest point, the jowl area. Also note eye position and crown of head. Head has elongated shape like an egg.

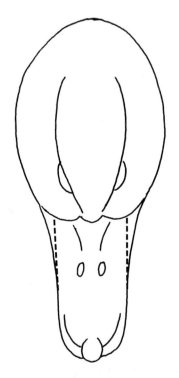

Wide Neck

The wedge. Common error is to make bill flare out as in the drawing, instead of coming into the head straight (dotted lines). This guy looks as though he would be capable of supersonic speed with that wedge shape. He might hit Mach 3 in level flight or a dive.

Correct top view of diving duck. Note head is wider toward the back than dabbling duck head, but still has the egg shape to it. Bill still comes into head straight and then head flares out. Be aware that tapered shape of bill can vary from one species to another.

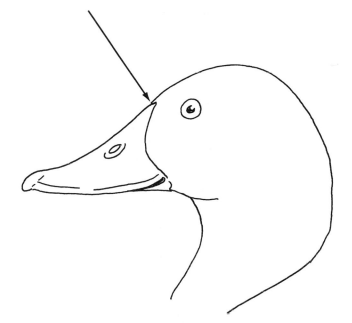

High brow and eye position. Another common error is to carve bill too high up on forehead area. Again, research will eliminate this error.

Eye position too far back.

Eye position too high.

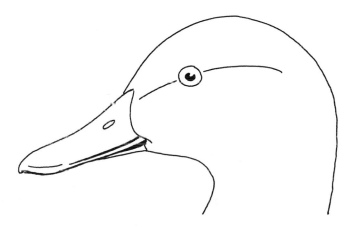

Correct eye position in eye channel.

No chin duck. Arrow indicates where chin was drawn too flat.

Dabbler (teal) on left, diver (ruddy duck) on right. Compare leg positions: Dabbler's legs are closer to center of body to accommodate walking on land. Diver's legs are farther back, placing feet in ideal position for swimming underwater.

This side profile of a widgeon shows important information: position of shoulder to neck; position of side pocket area; distance between end of side pockets and start of tail; and head and neck pulled back and positioned between shoulders.

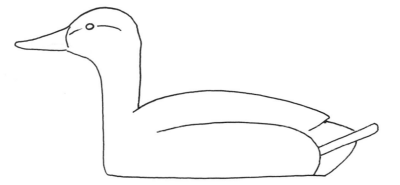

This little guy has some definite problems. He has no breast area in the front. It would be nice to give him some chest and neck area with his head back. His shoulders are too far ahead and his side pocket area is too low and long. There is no room between end of side pockets and start of tail.

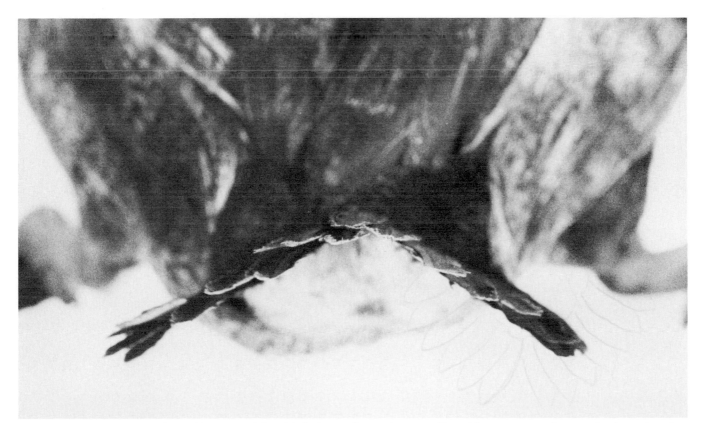

This view of tail feathers from the rear of the bird shows the stair-step effect. You can see the top feather showing like a top step. And you can go down steps either way.

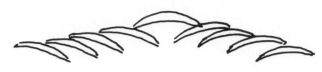

A common mistake—the feathers are carved slanting the wrong way—down on the uphill side. There is also no camber, or tent shape, to the feathers as shown in the "stair-step" photograph.

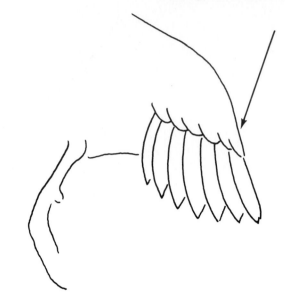

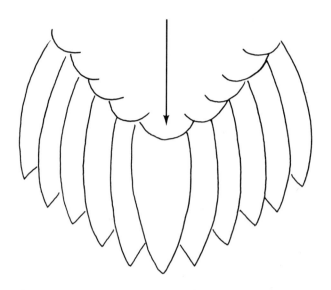

Flaps down for landing. Tail is bent down to slow flight.

This top view of a tail partially folded gives the appearance that there is one center feather. That is because the tail folded covers another feather below the center feather. The tail in fact has a left half and a right half that operate like ailerons on an airplane.

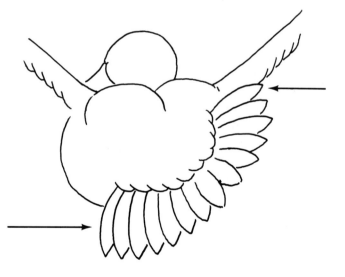

Starting a turn, bird uses tail like ailerons on an airplane. Note that right half of tail is turned up, whereas left half of tail is still down.

Tail open all the way, showing both halves with no apparent center feather.

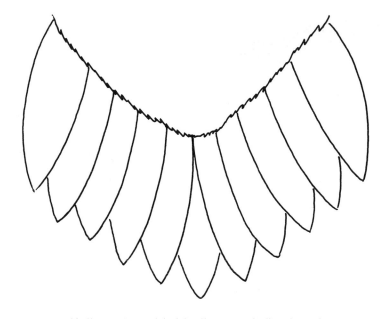

Bottom view of tail feathers partially closed.

2

Making the Pattern

To beginning and even experienced carvers pattern making can be very confusing at times. But no matter how you look at it, the key to a successful carving is how well you construct your initial pattern. This means opening your eyes and your mind to fully research what you will be carving. Of course, you can always take the easy way out and use one of the excellent pattern books that are on the market. But, eventually, you will resign yourself to the fact that if you are to grow as a carver, you will have to design your own patterns.

The first question we know that you will ask is, "How do I obtain good research material to create a good pattern?" You can start your own research center by cutting out photographs from outdoor publications that feature bird photographs; obtaining field guides and ornithology books; and visiting a game farm or zoo and taking your own photographs. You can also obtain excellent photographs from wildlife photographers. Many of them sell their pictures at carving shows.

If you're a duck hunter or know of someone who is, obtain study skins or have them mounted. A good taxidermist can be of great benefit. We do not, however, advise you to carve or make patterns directly from a mounted specimen, as taxidermists too are susceptible to making mistakes, just as we are. But a good mounted specimen can be invaluable. There are also many universities that have an ornithology department with mounts and study skins on hand. If you have one in your area, check it out.

You'll find that in a relatively short period of time you will have acquired a substantial collection of valuable research material. Catalog everything according to species and keep adding to your collection.

With enough reference material for a particular species, you're ready to create your pattern. It doesn't matter whether you are

Camera equipment can include a motorized winder and a telephoto lens (100 to 300 MM shown).

A quality-mounted bufflehead hen.

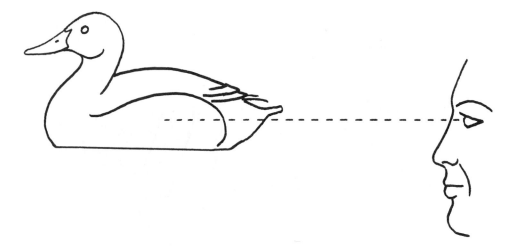

A good side profile should be photographed almost at eye level.

Although this is a nice photograph, it doesn't lend itself to a good pattern. The bird was photographed on an angle, creating a distorted profile which would result in a confusing and distorted carving.

This is what we're looking for—a true side profile that will help you to create a good pattern.

Use an opaque projector to enlarge photographs or magazine pictures to life-size.

working from a slide or a photograph, but a true side profile is essential. You'll need to enlarge your side profile with either a slide projector or an opaque projector (for photographs or magazine pictures). If you have neither of these projection devices, you can always use a line graph. This enables you to enlarge pictures or illustrations by using squares. Say, for instance, that you would like to enlarge a photograph. You would draw the grid as shown. If the squares measure ½ inch, you can enlarge your graph by making the grid larger; your formula might be ½ inch equals 1 inch.

Now that you have the means to enlarge your photograph or slide, enlarge it to life-size. *Life-size?* How are you to enlarge something to life-size if you don't know how large life-size is? This is where one of the great inventions of the carving world comes in: the *study bill*. This plaster or plastic study aid is an invaluable tool. (Study bills are advertised for sale in just about all of the carving catalogs.)

When a bird dies, moisture is lost from its

bill, thereby shrinking it. Under no circumstances should you use the measurements from a mounted specimen or a study skin. A study bill, however, is taken from a mold of the duck's bill, before it has had a chance to shrink. Thus, the study bill is an accurate tool for measurement. And with the knowledge that each species has bill measurements varying within a fraction of an inch of each other, it is safe to assume that if the bill of a mallard averages 2½ inches in length, our enlargement of the slide, photograph, or graph drawing should be in proportion. If you enlarge the projection of whatever species so that the projected length is the same

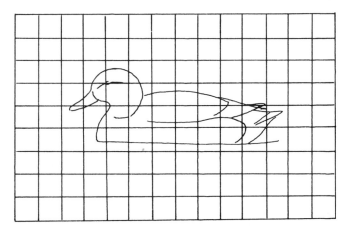

Line graph. Enlarge the squares and re-draw the shape in the appropriate squares.

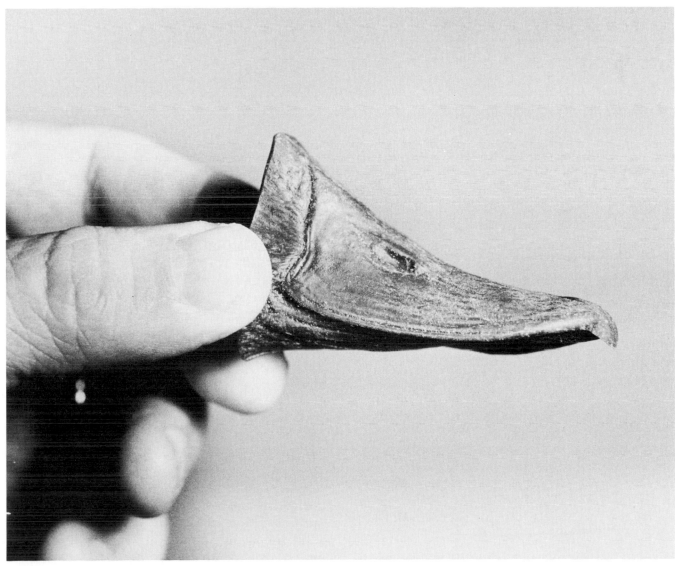

Study bill, drake redhead.

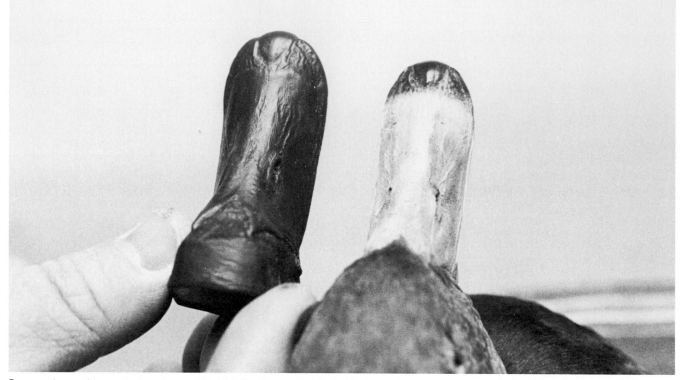

Comparison of mounted redhead bill (right) with study bill (left) of the same species. Notice difference in size — mounted bill has shrunk.

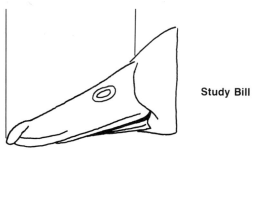

Study Bill

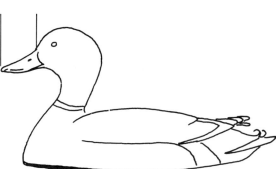

Enlarge projection so that projected bill is same length as study bill.

length as the study bill, everything else should be in proportion. To clarify this further, if the average length bill of mallard drakes is 2½ inches long, and if you stay within a fraction of an inch of that length, you probably will be correct in the bill length of other mallard drakes. This reasoning also holds true with other species.

Having made your enlargement life-size, trace the side profile. Tracing it on a firm piece of cardboard or paper will keep the pattern less susceptible to tears and make it easier to trace around when transferring the pattern to wood.

Now that you've completed the side profile, your next step is to create a top view. This is perhaps the most difficult part of your pattern-making endeavors, since most birds are pretty alert when a human being is standing over them. If you're fortunate enough to live near a game farm or zoo with a bridge walkway, you'll be able to obtain some very useful top shots. Or, if you raise your own birds, you can devise ways to pho-

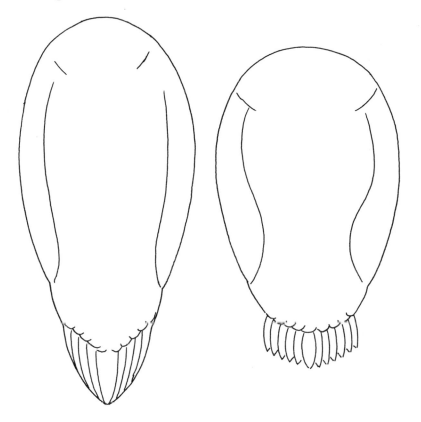

Comparison of body shapes, top view. Dabbler (left) looks like an elongated teardrop; diver (right) appears more rounded and compact.

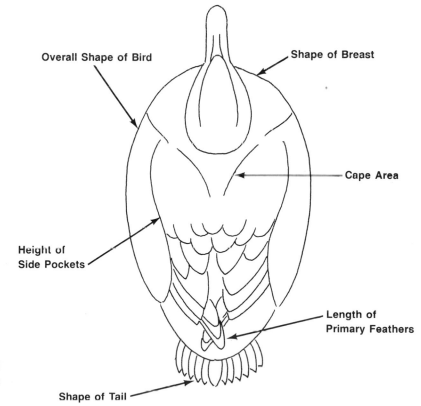

Overall Shape of Bird

Shape of Breast

Cape Area

Height of
Side Pockets

Length of
Primary Feathers

Shape of Tail

Here are some of the anatomical features you should be aware of and take notes on when creating your top view pattern.

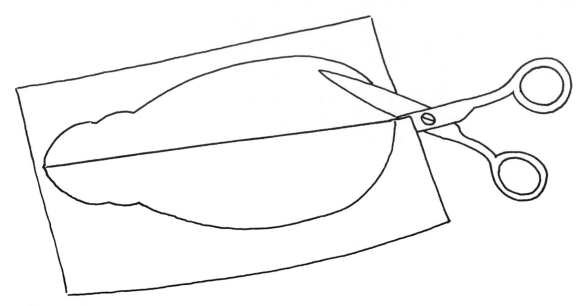

Once you've completed top view, draw a line straight through center and cut out one half.

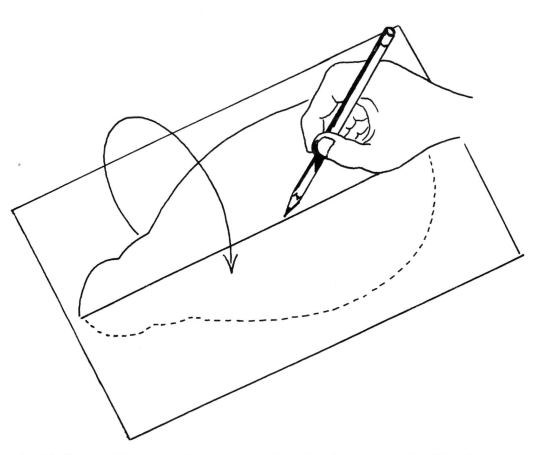

Position this cut-out half on another piece of paper or cardboard and trace around it. Then flip it over and draw the other side. This gives you a balanced pattern to work from.

A developed pattern, top view and side view, using drawing to develop feather shapes and light and dark areas.

Another preliminary study pattern of side profile of redhead hen.

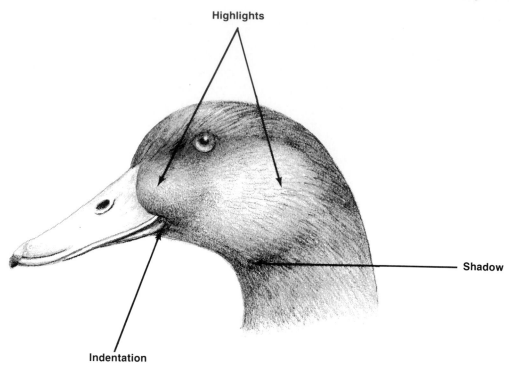

Highlights

Shadow

Indentation

Use your sketches as a notebook. Also write down features that catch your eye and that can be later applied to your carving.

A Ben Schmidt decoy. This is the type of decoy that decorative carvings have evolved from.

tograph them from the top. These shots are, unfortunately, hard to come by and must be improvised most of the time.

Now that you have created your pattern, top and side views, all you have to do is trace it on the wood and cut it out, right? Wrong! We would like to carry it a step further. We would like you to learn (if you don't already know) how to draw. You don't have to be an accomplished artist to create useful drawings; but you will eventually have to put all that you see into your carving.

Most good, flat-medium artists take the time to plan their compositions with numerous preliminary sketches. In essence, they are making and correcting their mistakes before they begin painting. You too can develop ideas and eliminate mistakes if you take the time to prepare before you start carving.

Draw in such areas as bulges, indentations, feather flow, highlights, shadows, and everything else that you deem important. Make notes on your sketches, and go into your carving with a definite plan of attack. It is much easier at this point to correct something, rather than try to add wood to your carving after the mistake has been made.

Decorative carving has evolved from a craft to fine art, and you're on your way to being an artist. Be innovative yet accurate in your patterns. Dwell upon the knowledge that you have already accumulated, and continually strive for that perfect carving.

3

Transferring the Pattern to Wood

Once you have made your pattern, cut it out and place the side profile or top view against the end of the block of wood. The most commonly used woods are basswood, tupelo, and jelutong because of their texture and grain. These three types are generally free of knots. If you have a long enough piece of wood, move back from the end of the block an inch or so and draw a line with a square. If the wood is checked or split, this should get you away from these problems. Put your pattern squarely against the line or end of the block and trace around it. Allow 1 inch on both sides of the block of wood for surplus or cut-off areas. You only need ¼ of an inch excess for the side profile.

Next, do the same with the other part of the pattern, making sure it also is squarely against the end of the block or the squared line you drew. It is extremely important to check to see that both patterns are against the end of the block or against the line. If not, your block will not come out well when you cut it on the band saw.

For the head pattern, follow the same procedure and make sure you use a good flat piece of wood in case you want to drill the eyes on a drill press after you cut out the head. If the block is crooked, the eyes may not come out even on both sides where drilled.

Once you've drawn the head and body pattern on the blocks of wood, you might want to mark your patterns and save them for future use. We usually destroy our patterns and try to make a better set for the next carving. This forces you to do more research, and you will usually pick a different position to carve as a result.

A rough-carved bird from a pattern drawn on the top and side of the blocks of wood. Note that patterns on body top and side are butted up to end of block.

4

Cutting Out the Pattern

After your pattern has been transferred, you are ready to cut the pattern from the top view first. We usually start at the tail area first, but it doesn't matter if you choose the front, or breast, area.

If you are fortunate enough to own a band saw, your cutting chore will be much easier. But don't be discouraged if you do not own one. There are other tools you can use. The hand-held electric jig saw will do a nice job, but you will need to clamp the block of wood down to a table to hold it in place. This will let you use both hands on the saw to guide your cut. The coping saw is another alternative. It is harder to use than the jig saw or band saw, but it will get the job done. Other

acceptable tools are the plain old hand axe, draw knife, or handsaw, or you can just carve all the excess with a knife.

Cutting any wood requires a good sharp blade and a certain amount of common sense about safety precautions, such as wearing safety eye glasses and keeping your fingers clear. Check your hardware on the right blade for your saw. We use a one-quarter-inch wide blade with four to six teeth per inch. The fewer the teeth, the less sawdust you have to load up in the saw cut. The blade is one-quarter-inch wide to enable you to cut around corners. A wider blade will make this task difficult.

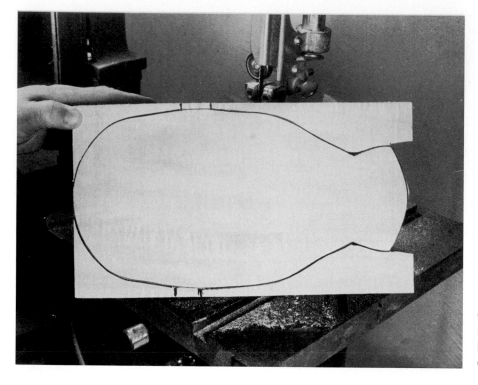

As we cut around tail, we will cut in around the curve to the areas marked and back out the blade. These marked areas hold the side profile on. Next, cut straight in to where you left off on the other cut. This will allow a wedge to come out, which will make it easier later to back out your blade. Be careful! Back the blade out of the cut. Shut off the saw and back it out if it gets stuck. Continue on to halfway point. Stop here and back out. Then do same on other side.

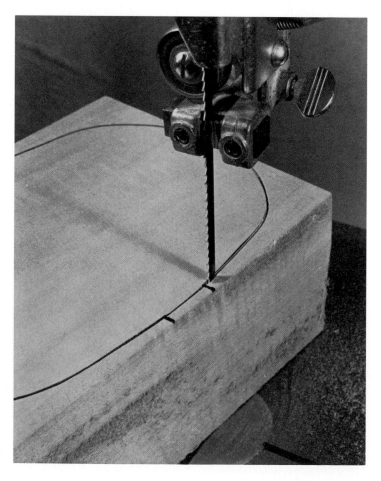

Reverse block and cut in from breast to halfway point. Leave about one inch uncut area on both sides.

Turn block on side to cut side profile. Now you see why the wood was left intact. This gives a nice flat area to cut on. An optional method is to cut both sides off and nail or tape them back on to put flat area back intact. Cut side profile completely off and go back and finish cutting off sides.

Tilt the table on the band saw and trim excess wood from sides and bottom. This saves a lot of carving later.

The same procedure we use for the body pattern can work for the head pattern.

You are cutting a smaller block of wood with the head, so watch your fingers. Drill eye holes if preferred.

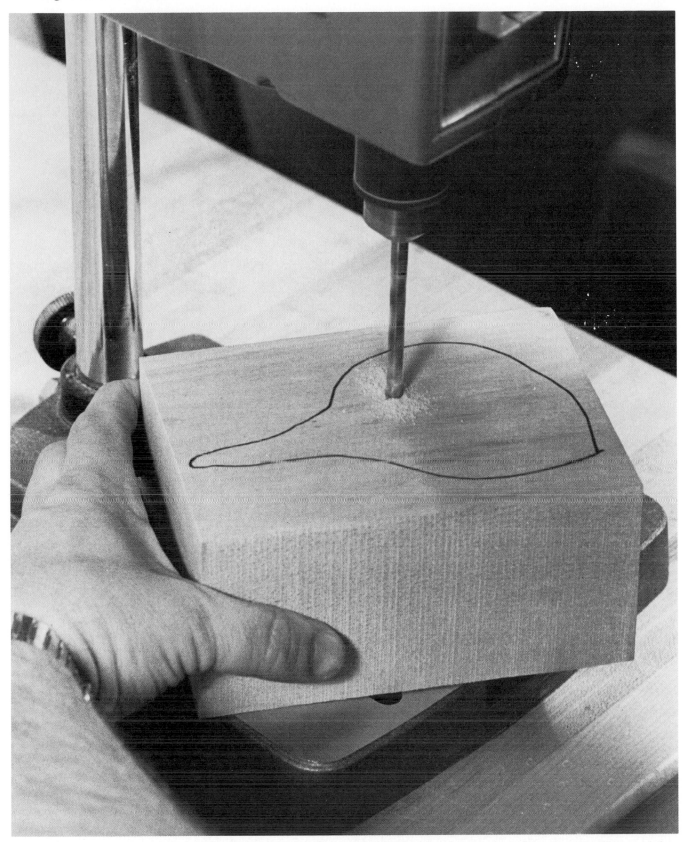

Drilling eye holes on drill press. Block of wood has been planed flat to insure that is level prior to drilling and that eye holes will come out even.

Drawing top view prior to cutting. Note bottom of block still attached to give flat surface to cut on.

Cutting top view of head.

5

Carving the Head

It is the head of a good carving that carries the life-like look, or animation, of the waterfowl. Needless to say, judges in competitive shows placc great importance in the head area.

We choose to carve the head as a separate piece of wood. The advantage to this is the ease with which you can handle and work the head. The disadvantage is the attachment of the head to the body. Unless you are very careful, a neck or joint line will show. Some carvers choose to carve the body and head as one piece for this very reason.

No matter how you choose to carve the head, you still need the basic guidelines we are going to draw. A study bill is used for drawing the bill lines, and a pair of calipers will enable you to measure and transfer to your carving these and other essential lines.

You'll also be using an Xacto knife and grinder for the intricate carving steps.

It's important to take great care in, among other steps, the installation of the eyes. We'd like to make a few recommendations on tools and supplies to make this process easier. For boring the eye holes, you can use a regular drill bit or the more expensive Forstner bits. Most drills tend to chip the wood around the eye holes, so we prefer to use a cone-shaped ruby carver or diamond carver. And for filling the holes, we recommend Elmers Professional Wood Filler. Other fillers may be used, such as plastic wood or wood dough or even two-part plumbers epoxy. We use Elmers because it is watcr solublc, thus enabling us to mold the eyelid area later on with a sable brush.

As always, good reference material is important, especially in the installation of the eyes. Use either an excellent mount or a photo showing a true side profile blown up to life-size.

One basic point to keep in mind when you begin: a diver has a thicker head at the back and jowl areas than does a dabbler. The can-vasback, for example, has a very thick neck and wide head (hence the nickname "Bull Neck Can"). If you have done the necessary research, you will have a block of wood for the head that may be nearly three inches thick for a canvasback. A dabbler head may be an inch or so narrower in most cases.

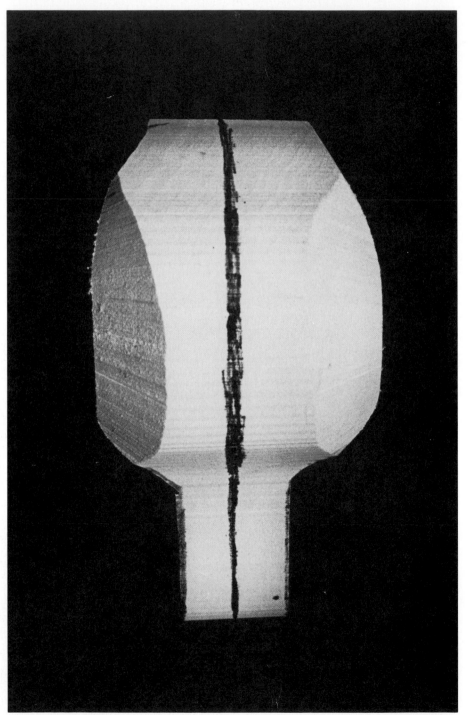

First step is to draw guide lines on top of head and bill and under bill. Start with a center line down through bill, up the head, and down back of head.

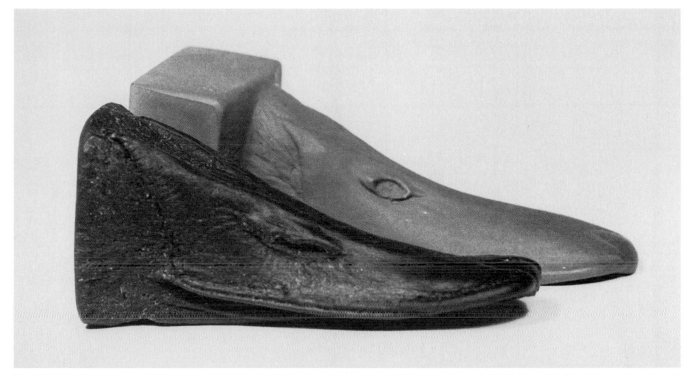

Next lines to lay out are bill lines. In order to do this properly, you should have a study bill. Pictured in front is a canvasback (diver) bill and in back, a mallard (dabbler) bill, both drakes.

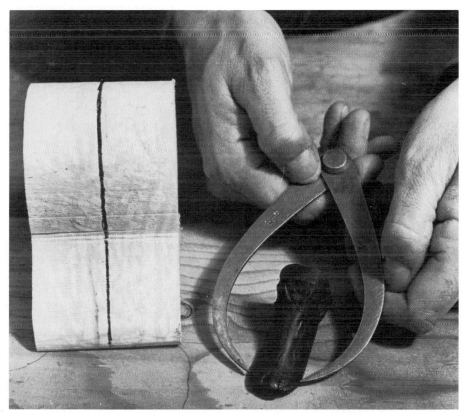

With calipers, measure width of study bill at widest point (near end of bill). Make marks on both sides of center line near end of bill and again close to head where bill goes into cheek area.

Transfer measurement to block and mark it.

Next, measure study bill from tip of nail up to tip of notch.

Transfer measurement to the block and mark top measurement by drawing a line across bill, to form a 'T' with center line.

Cross line drawn on bill. From this cross line to end of block will be your bill length.

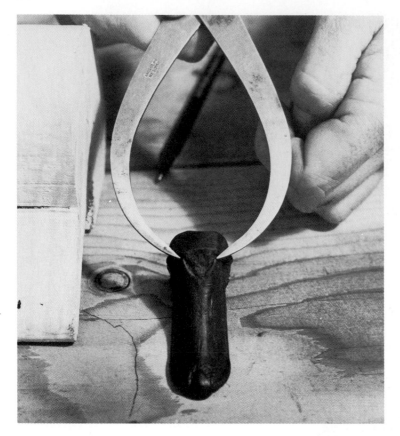

Measure width of notch on study bill.

Notch drawn on block.

Notch and bill lines drawn on.

Now at the notch you will start draw-ing the crown lines, on top of the head. Compare top of duck head on the right to block of wood with lines drawn. You will now see the need for guidelines to get correct width proportions. From notch in the bill, draw your lines back in an egg-shaped pattern on both sides of cen-ter line as in the picture.

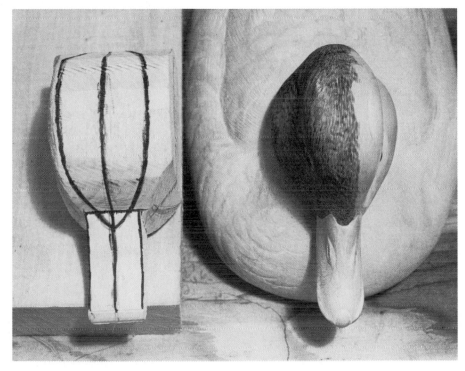

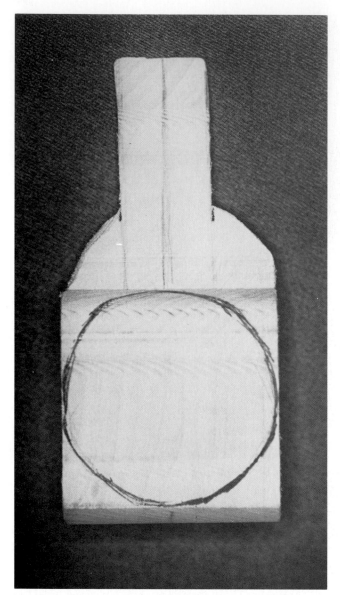

Next guidelines are on bottom of neck area. Here we will draw a circle and leave it as wide as possible. Excess trimming will be done later when we attach head to body.

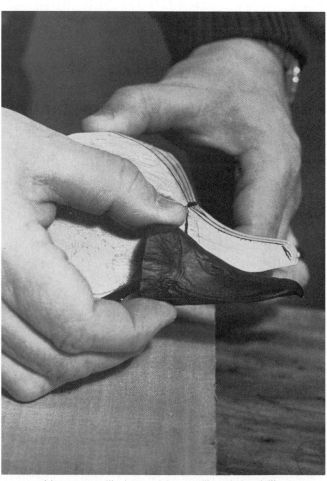

Now we will draw side profile of the bill.

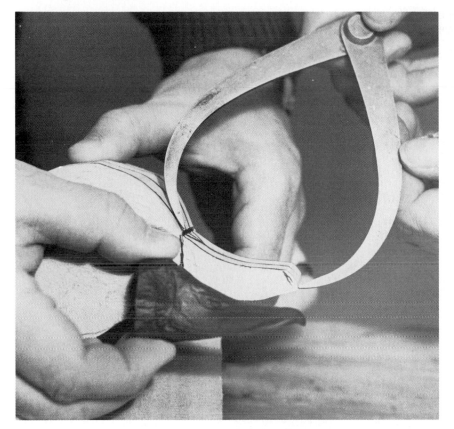

Measure from tip of bill to point of notch and mark that point on side of bill.

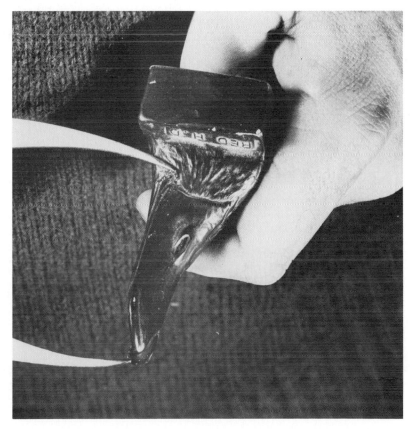

Measure from tip of bill to side or separation between upper and lower mandible, and mark side of bill with a line.

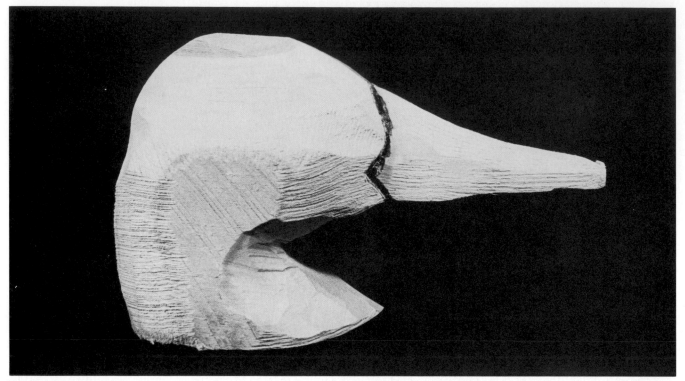

Next, draw cheek line down from notch to bottom of lower mandible. Look at study bill carefully before you attempt to draw this line.

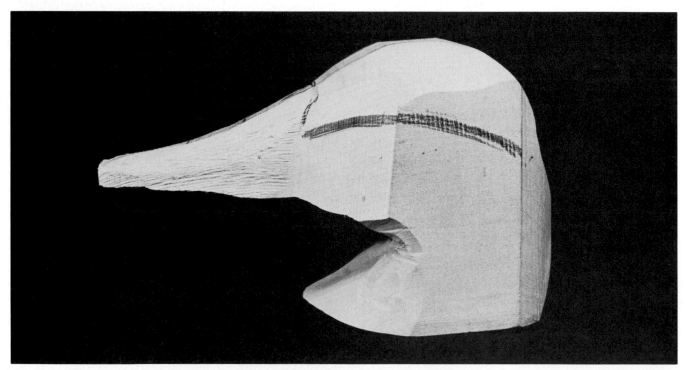

The last reference line will be the eye channel line, which curves from edge of bill back through eye area. If you like to drill a hole through the head with a drill press to make a small eye hole, make sure that your head stock is planed flat so that eye holes will match up on both sides.

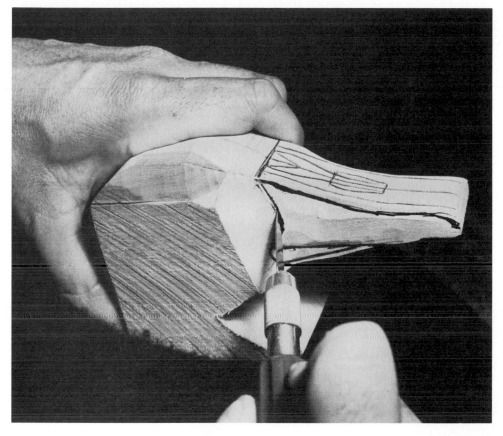

Now we can begin carving with an Xacto knife. Starting with cheek line, cut straight down on check line. Cut as deep as possible without straining blade. Repeat this until you have cut about ⅛ inch deep.

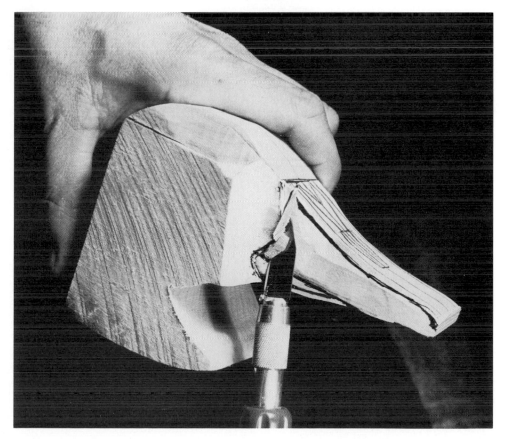

Now back cut to cheek with knife until wood pops out.

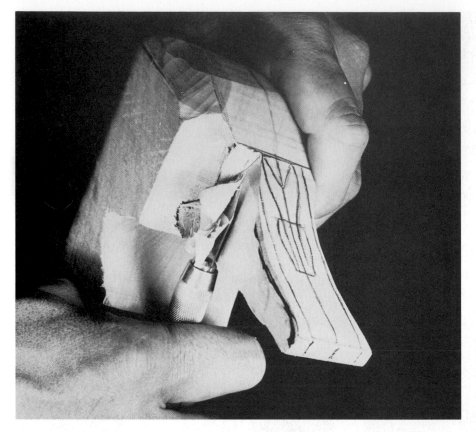

Repeat these steps until you have cut all the way up to bill notch on top and bill's widest point drawn on bottom of bill. Turn over head and do the same to other side. When you are done, you should have a straight, wide bill.

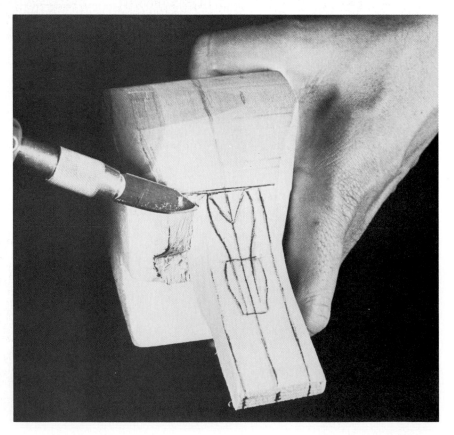

Knife showing how much has been cut out to get up to notch. Leave a little excess below notch on side of bill about where point of knife is.

The grinder, with 44B handpiece and ¾-inch cone-shaped carbide tip, is the tool needed for the next step —cutting the eye channel.

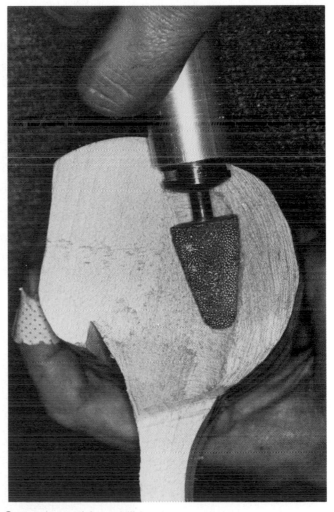

Cut a channel from bill back through eye towards back of head.

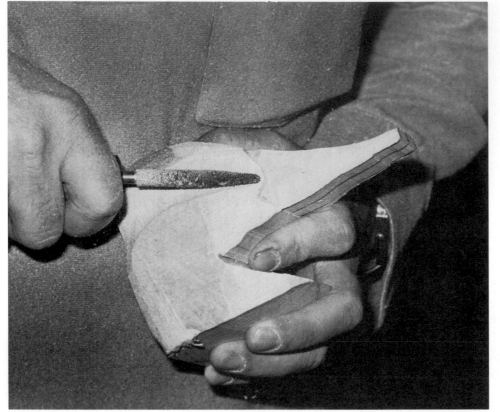

Grinding with long, tapered cutter to make a narrow channel.

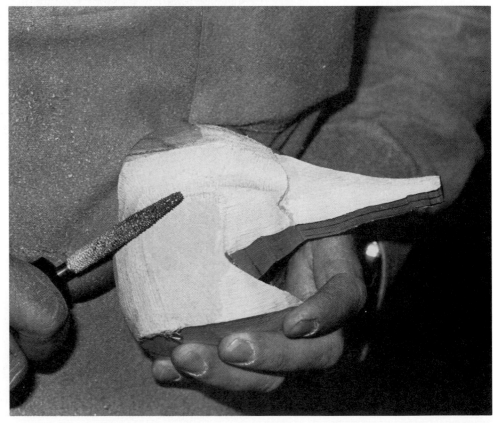

Continue cutting eye channel toward back of head. Note that channel is *curved*, not straight.

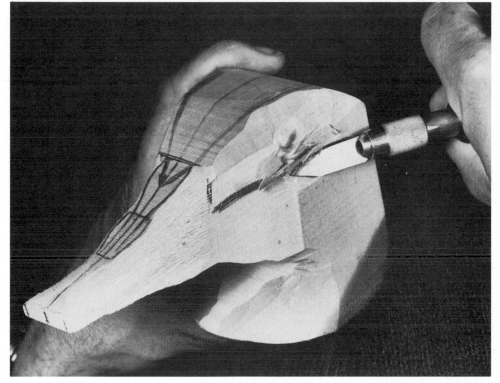

Cutting eye channel with an Xacto knife. Note shape of blade, it is sharp on one edge and tapers to a point. The round edge with a point is easiest to use compared to a flat edge or rounded point.

Front view showing eye channel before next procedure—grinding up to crown line on top of head.

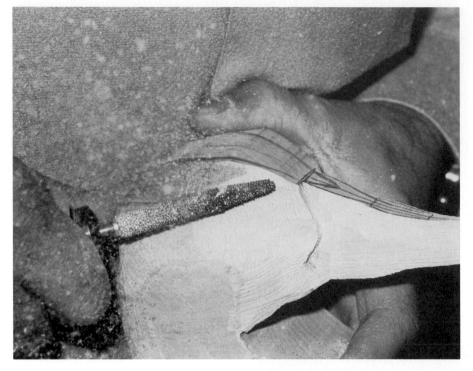

Use grinder to clean out eye channel from top and bottom. Duplicate procedure on other side of head. Always check your carving from top, back, and front views to insure a symmetrical carving. Without stopping to check, you might end up with top of head crooked or one cheek higher than the other. The eye channel area from the center can be cleaned out right up to the lines we have drawn from the crown of the head.

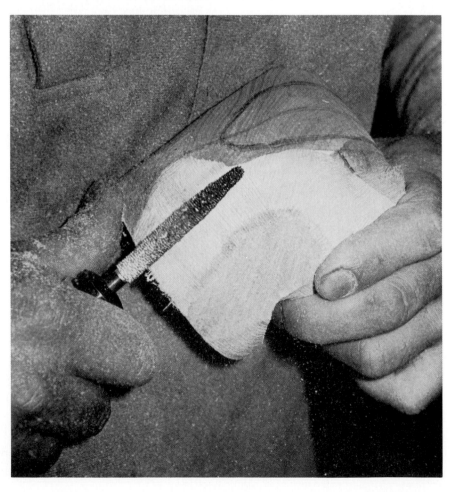

Next, start rounding off back of head and lower neck area around to the center line. Note that on this canvasback, the back will be wide and blunt.

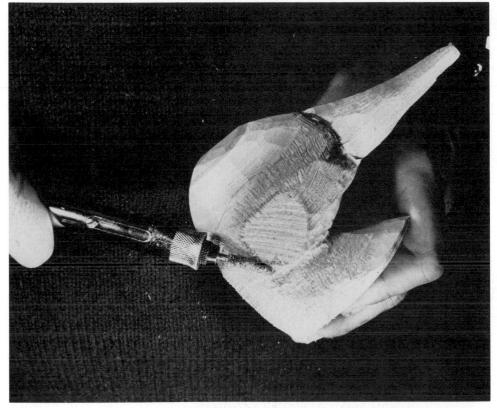

When rounding out the neck area, bring out back of the cheek, or jowl, area by grinding up from neck in an arc towards top of head. From the back side of that arc, carve wood away by rounding towards back of head. Repeat this procedure on other side of head.

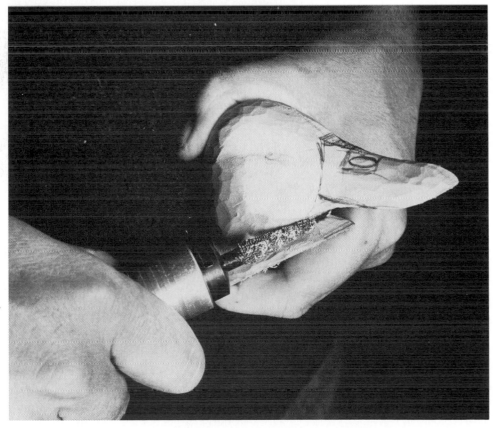

Grinding neck area on a teal. (Note smaller, tapered carbide cutter to get under chin.) Round out neck area and leave it as thick as possible. Later we will temporarily attach head to body and carve neck to fit breast and shoulder area.

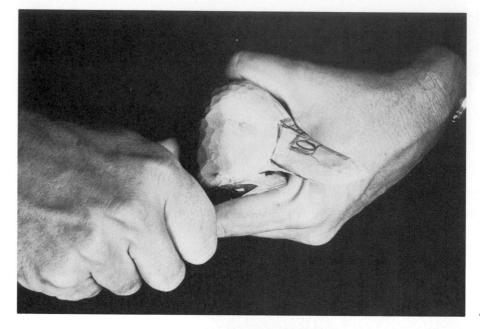

An Xacto knife can do the same job.

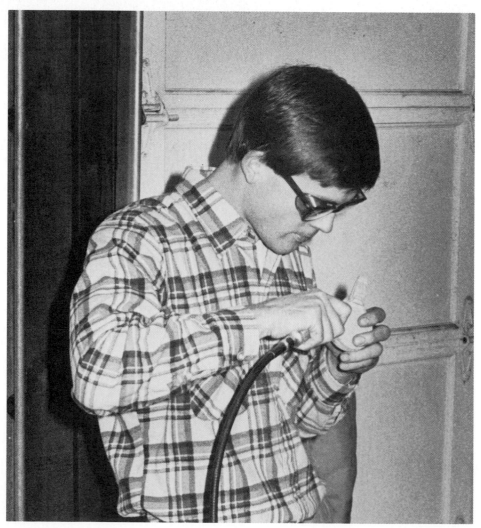

Grinding under chin area. Note safety glasses.

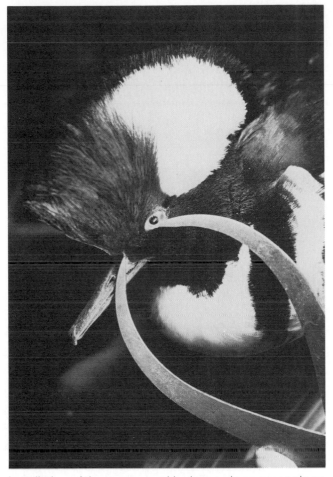

Installation of the eyes—a critical step since proper location is key to a good carving. Measure distance from front edge of cheek where bill joins head (point of notch) back to center of the eye, as shown on this hooded merganser. Look carefully at how low or high eye is in reference to top of head. Also note eye is closer to front of head than center from a side profile. Once you have located both eye positions, check from top of head and from front to see if they are even.

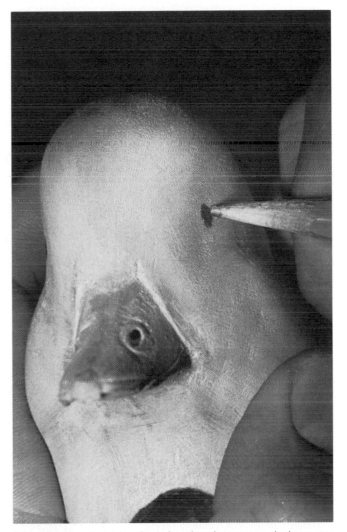

Measurement put in place by drawing around glass eye and filling in to solid dot, as shown on this bufflehead.

Once you've marked both eye positions, start boring eye holes. We prefer to use a cone-shaped ruby carver (pictured here) or diamond carver. With one of these tools, you can leave a neat hole by placing the eye in the hole intermittently until eye fits into hole.

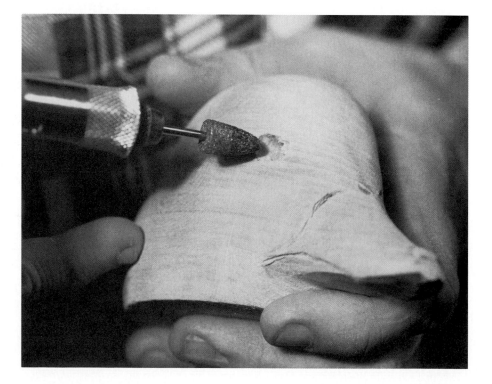

Boring hole has started.

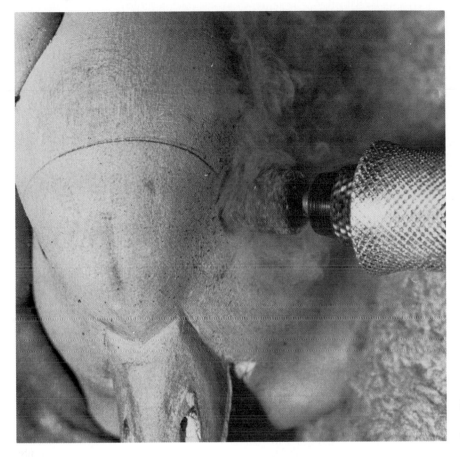

Smoke coming out of eye hole while being bored. Note reference line across top of head to center of other eye.

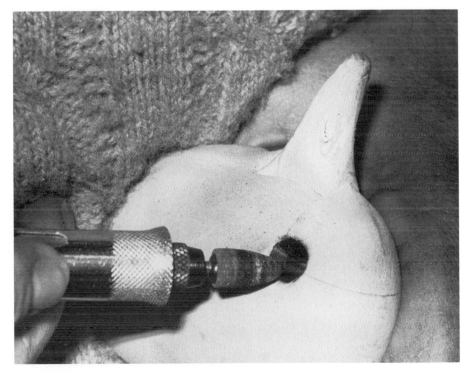

Eye hole bored to size. Use ruby carver or diamond carver to smooth out edges of hole to form eye socket.

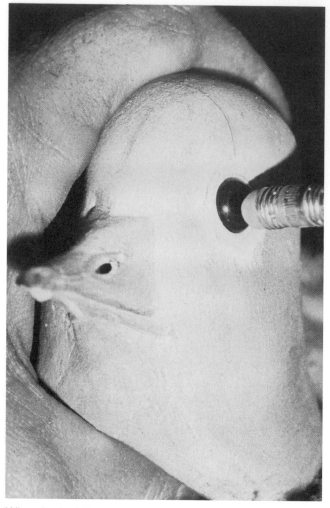

When both sides are completed, fill holes with wood filler such as Elmers Professional Wood Filler. Then place eye over hole and slowly push eye into hole until filler oozes out. We use a pencil eraser to push eye in because it does not slip off eye.

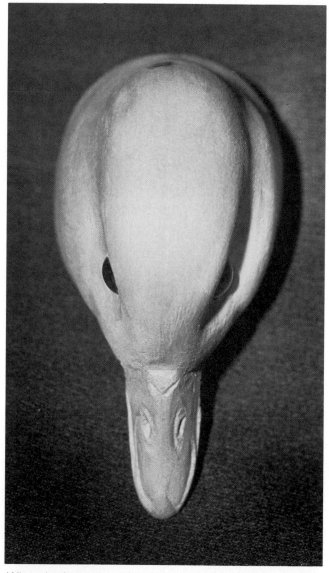

When both eyes are in place, check to make sure they are straight up and down when viewed from top of head, and that they slant towards the front.

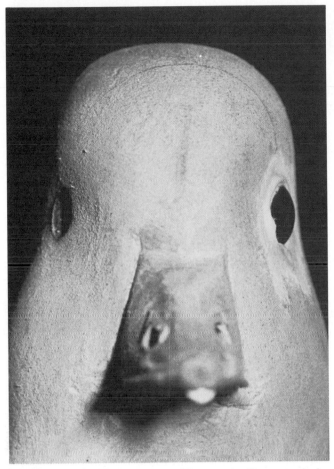

Front view showing eye position and other eye hole bored.

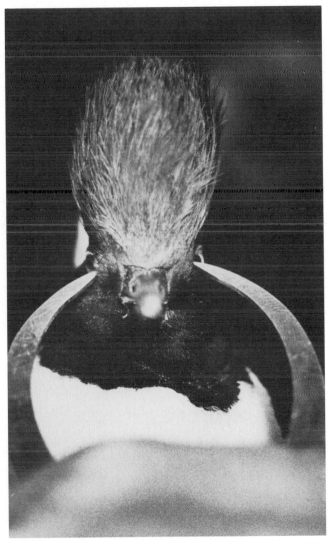

Make sure to measure between eyes to insure proper distance apart, as shown on this hooded merganser. The calipers will touch the skull, giving an accurate measurement.

Use sable brush with water to mold eyelid area. Keep brush wet when using water-soluble fillers.

In finishing the head, some accent lines are added in the front cheek area. The jowl line is drawn in on this old squaw drake. Note eyes marked but not yet installed.

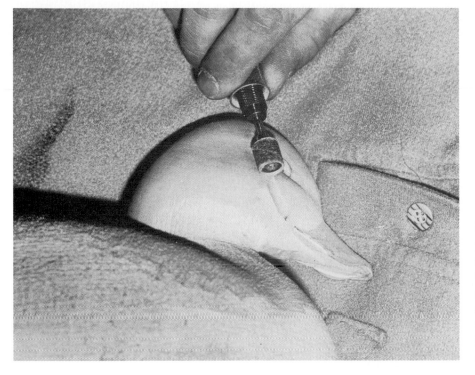

Using grinder with sanding drum to put in jowl line. Sand from below the eye downward and curving to bottom of bill. Smooth this area out and it will appear as a cheeky or puffy jowl area. Other lines can be added, depending on species you are carving, such as muscle tone lines to accent back of cheek.

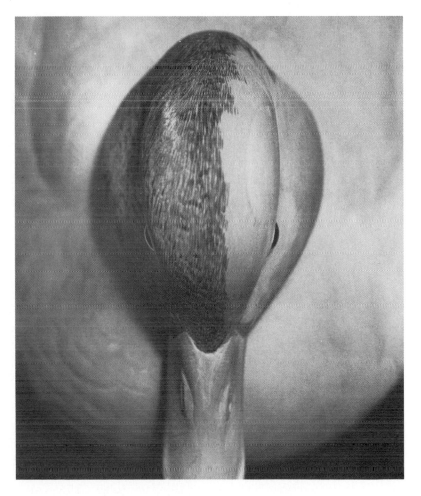

Top view of head completed, except for the bill and texturing, which we discuss in chapters 6 and 11.

6

Carving the Bill

Like the head, the bill is a crucial area that helps properly convey the attitude and animation of the subject you have chosen. The look in the eyes and character in the face are viewed with interest by most show judges so be careful to study this area in detail before you start. The bill detail can be tricky enough when it's carved in a closed position; but if it's carved in the open position there's more chance for error. If you're a novice carver, concentrate on a closed bill first.

The tools we use on the bill are the calipers again, the Foredom tool, the Xacto knife, and a simple tool used by carpenters called a contour shaper. The contour shaper will let you see how close the shape of your wood bill is to that of the study bill. It's important to be constantly comparing the two throughout your carving. Get used to holding the head at arm's length to eyeball the bill for straightness and accuracy in shape. Another trick is

to put the study bill next to the wood bill (side by side) and eyeball them to insure your side profile is correct. We keep two study bills; one is cut in half so we can place it flat on the wood to draw a good side profile. We also use a band saw to cut that bill along the cheek line, so the bill will fit against the head better.

Before you start carving, it's important to understand some facts about the waterfowl bills. If you study several bills of one species, such as a canvasback drake, you will note that the bills are not identical. They each will have different creases, lines, bumps, or holes. You might even relate this to fingerprints on humans. There are, however, very similar lines on the bills of most ducks. To the untrained eye, the lip area of the upper mandible appears to be one continuous line. Actually, this is not so; there is a lower line and an upper line near the tip of the bill. On the upper mandible at the front of the bill is a V- or U-shaped area called the *nail.* This is common on most ducks and geese. The nail area has a similar shape under the bill on the lower mandible.

The nostril area of most dabbling ducks and of most diving ducks seems to slant inward when viewed from the top. We say *most* because obviously we do not have research material on all the waterfowl. It seems fair at this point to say, do not take things for granted. Do your own research to be sure.

Check the bill of the subject you have chosen and really get acquainted with it. Look at the top, bottom, front, nail area, nostril area, and the notch where the forehead of the bird starts. (Point of interest—Normally on duck bills, there are two areas that are concave: under the nostrils, and at the lower edge of the upper mandible where the two halves of the bill join at the cheek area.)

Keeping all this in mind, let's begin the bill carving by adding some guidelines.

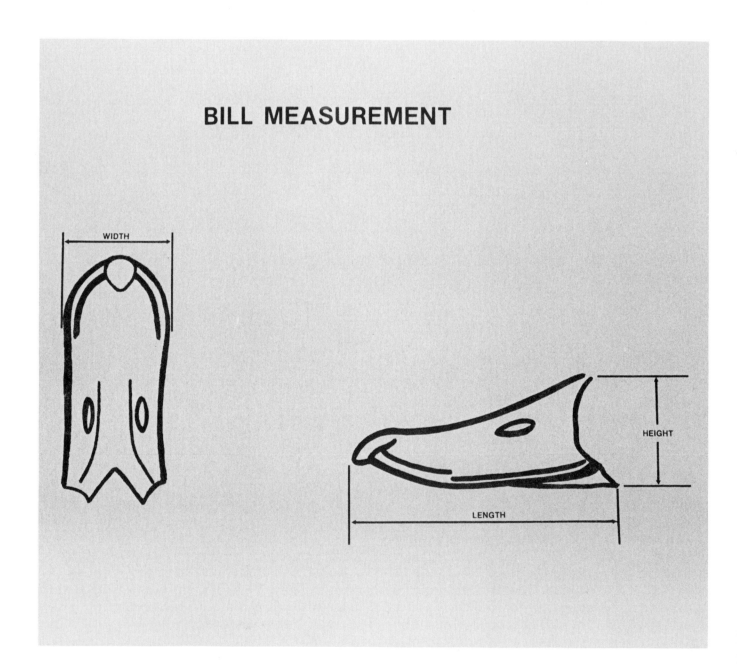

BILL MEASUREMENT

Two canvasback bills, both drakes.
Note difference in lines and nostrils.

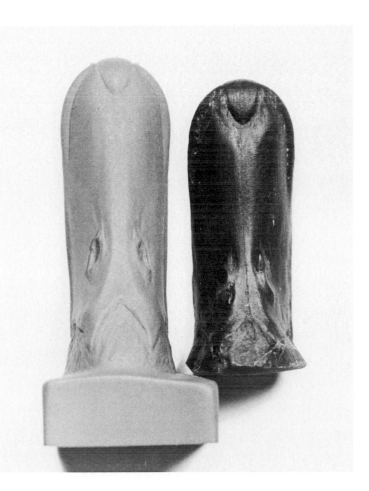

Two mallard bills, both drakes. Note difference in
length.

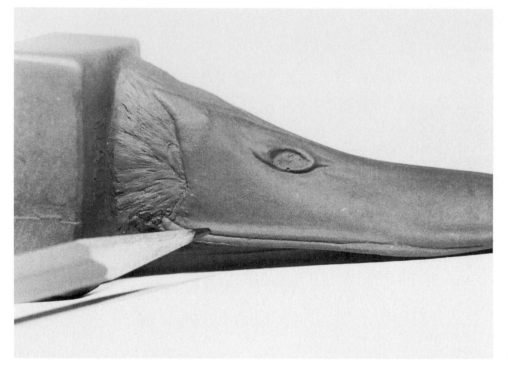

Note detail of lip-like line on bill.

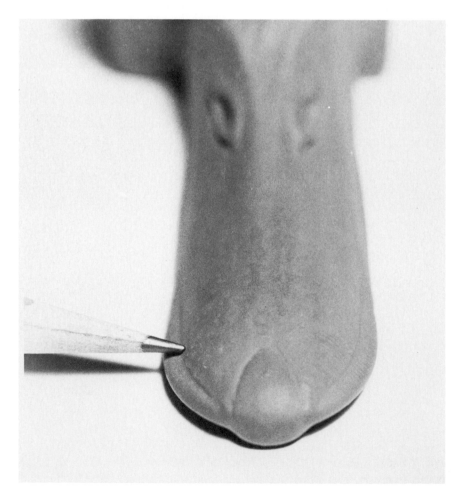

Upper lip area near front of bill.

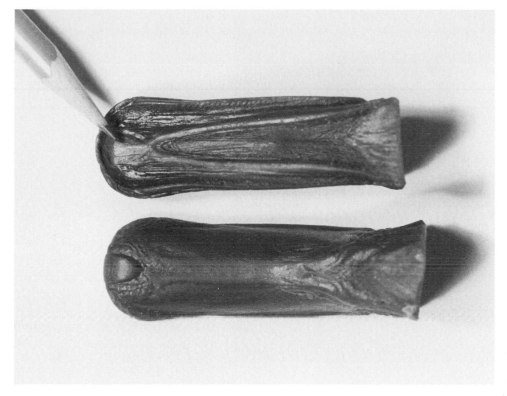

Same shape on lower mandible bottom as upper mandible nail area.

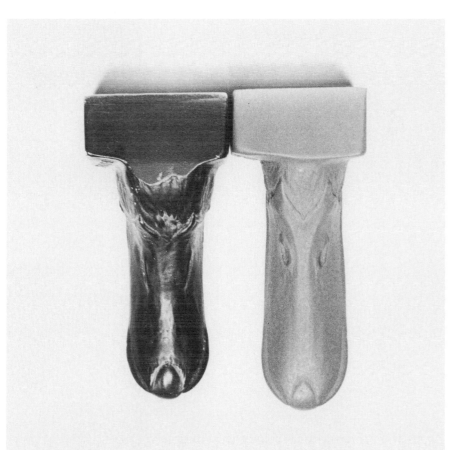

Note inward slant of nostrils due to shape of bill.

NORTHEAST COMMUNITY COLLEGE
LIBRARY/RESOURCE CENTER

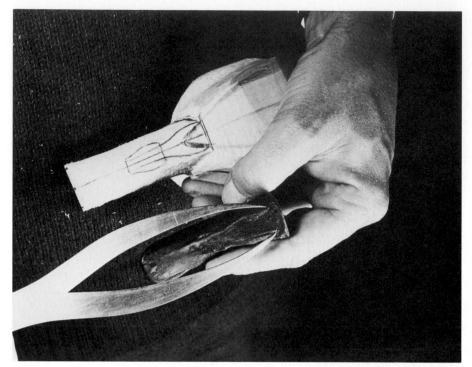

Use calipers to measure the width of the area above the nostrils that appears to be flat just in front of the notch, as well as the length. (Without guidelines, you might carve the bill pinched in this area.)

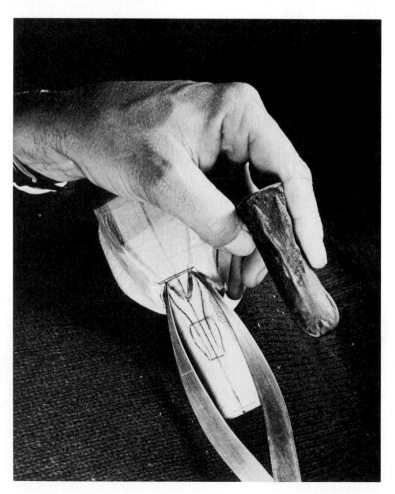

Transfer measurement from study bill to wood bill to the cheek width.

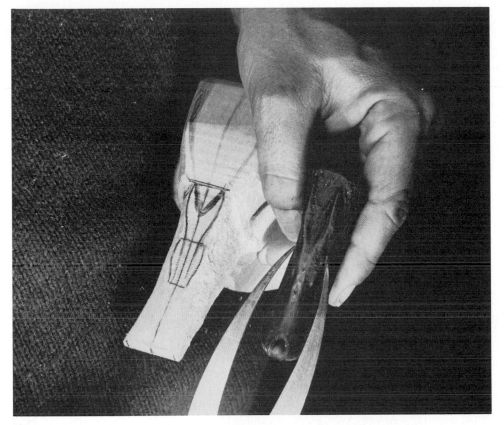

Measure nostril width of study bill.

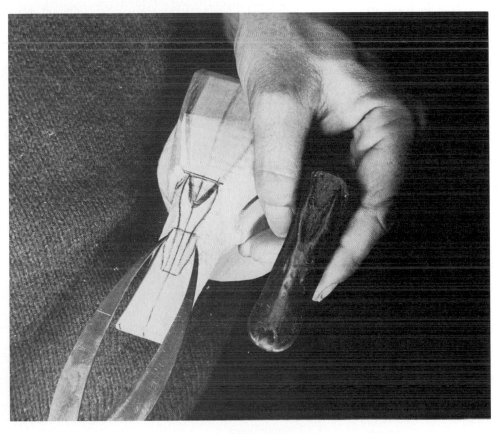

Transfer nostril width measurement to wood bill and draw nostril width lines.

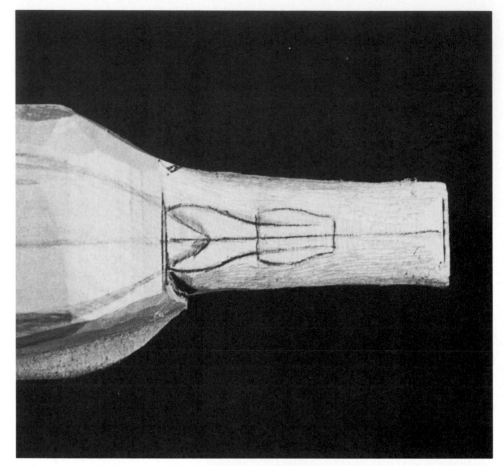

Bill width guidelines drawn on.

Use small, tapered cutter to cut up to guide lines on both sides, taking caution not to remove too much wood over the nostril area. You will want to leave some width in that area to carve the raised nostrils.

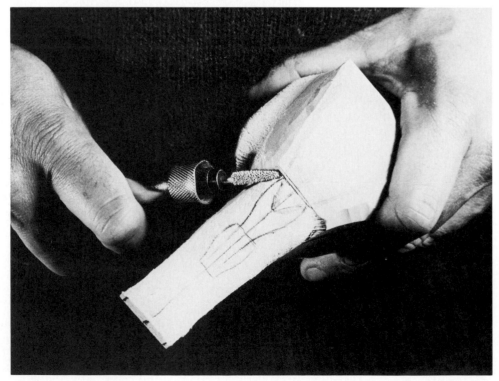

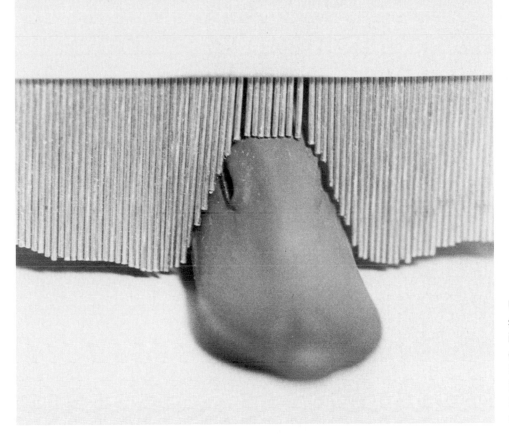

Use contour shaper to check study bill shape. Continue carving toward the end of the bill to get your basic shape. This part is tricky so we suggest you take it easy and start using the contour shaper to check your bill as often as possible.

Use contour shaper to check carved bill. Carve a little, stop and check again and again. Note the shape is very close to the study bill. When you carve the bill to the proper width where it goes into the head, check your guide lines under the bill also to insure you are carving a straight bill.

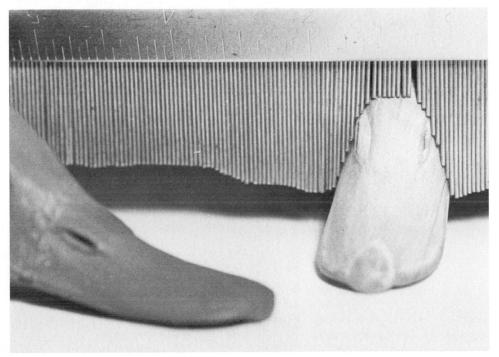

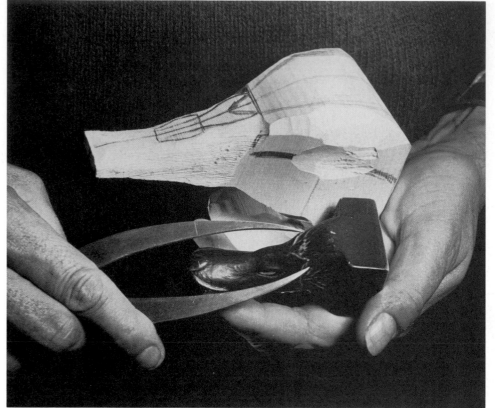

Starting at the top of the notch area, carve up to your guidelines. Use calipers to check periodically the thickness on the top of the bill.

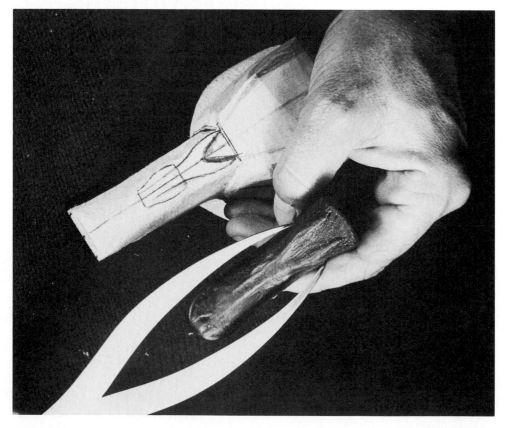

Measure width of study bill in the middle, where bill meets cheek.

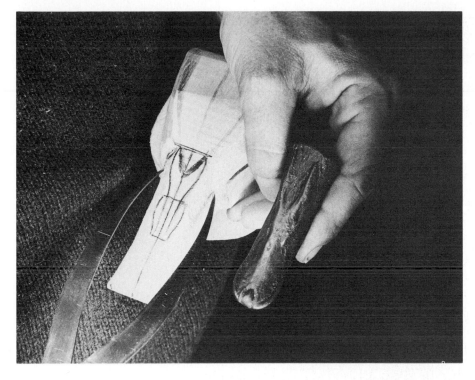

Check width of wood bill in the middle.

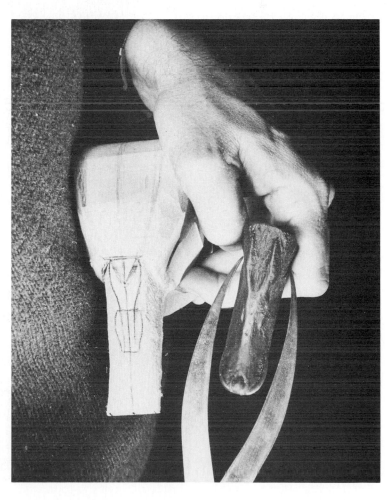

Check width of study bill at the bottom, the lower edge of upper mandible where it joins cheek. Then check wood bill. If you follow this procedure of measuring top, middle, and bottom areas, the bill will flow into the cheek area as it should and not be too skinny or flared out.

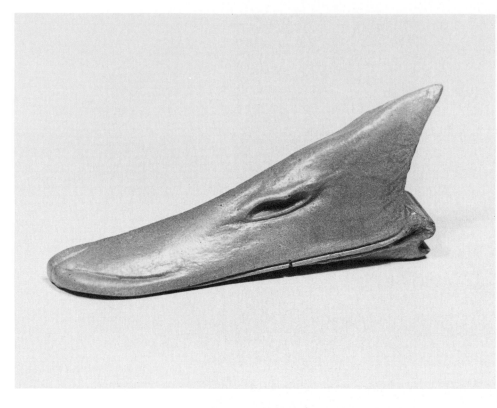

Study bill cut in half and cut around cheek area. Use it to check accuracy of side profile.

One-half study bill placed on wood bill to check shape of side profile.

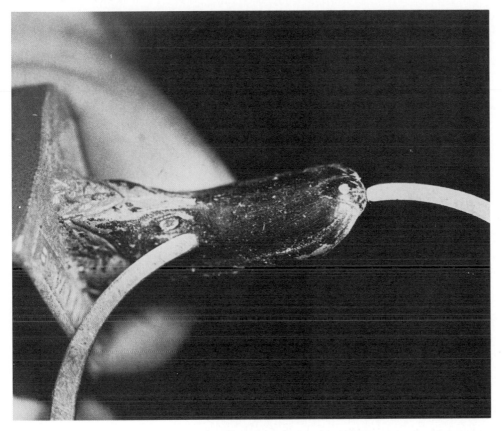

Now you should lay out the nostril area. This can be done by adding some more guide lines. With calipers, measure distance from tip of study bill to front edge of nostril lip area around nostril hole.

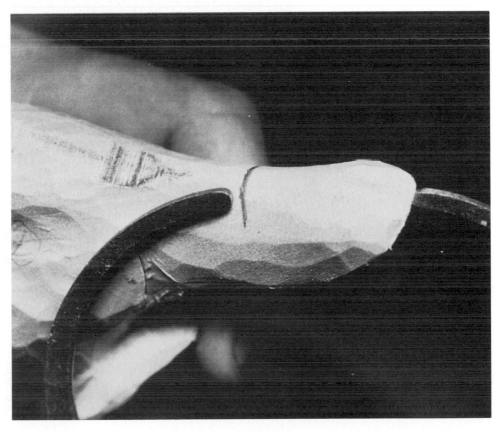

Transfer measurement to carved bill to front edge of nostril area. Make a mark on your bill and draw a line over the top of the bill.

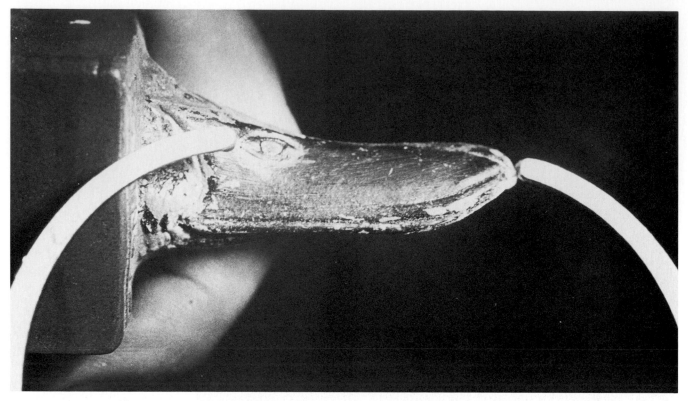

Next, measure from the tip of study bill to back lip area around nostril hole.

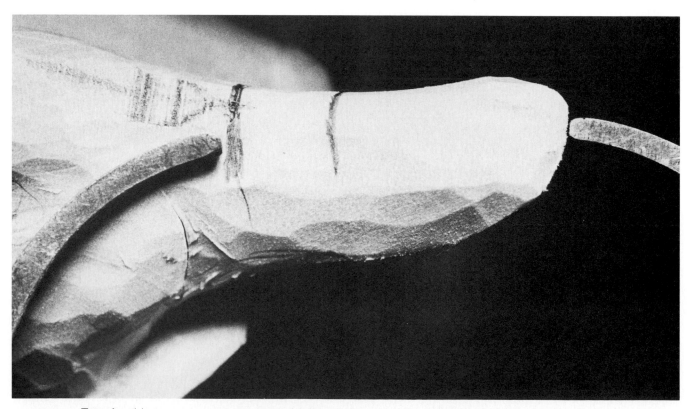

Transfer this measurement to carved bill and draw a line over the bill at the proper point.

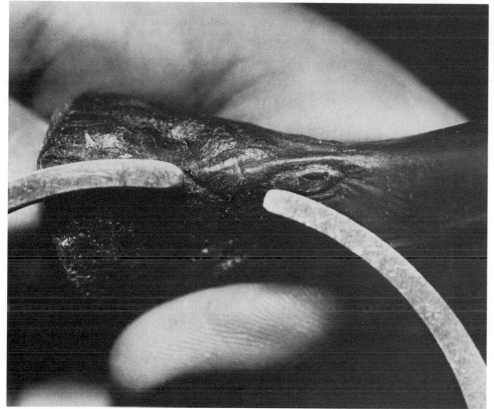

Next, as a check, measure from the rear edge of the lip area around the nostril hole to the point at the top of the bill to make sure of proper placement.

Check against measurement on carved bill.

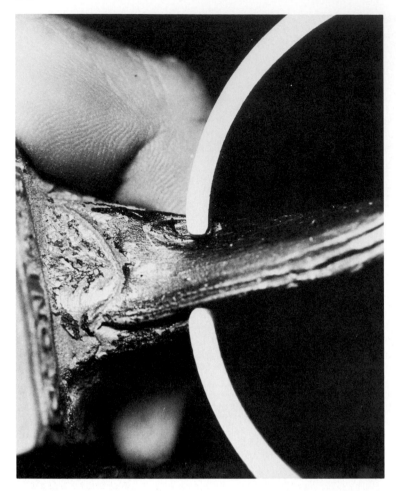

Now check the distance between the nostrils looking from the top down. Check the front and rear part of the nostrils.

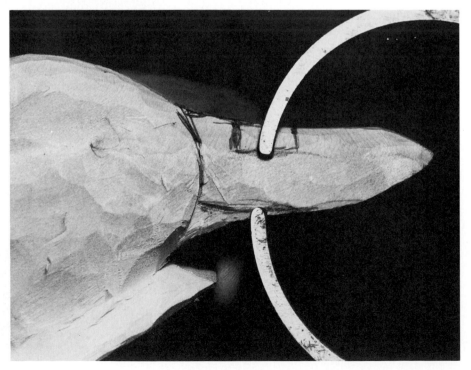

Then check from bottom edge of upper mandible to bottom edge of nostril area. This is a good habit to get into, the measuring of everything to insure accuracy in detail.

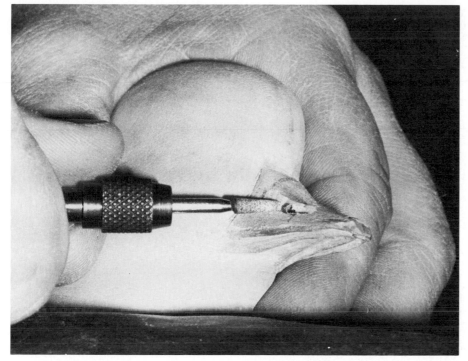

You can now carve nostril area by using a flexible shaft tool—a knife or files or a grinder with a ruby carver or diamond carver. The ruby or diamond carvers seem to work well for this area. They are easy to use and do not load up with sawdust. (Carving bit is red oxide stone.)

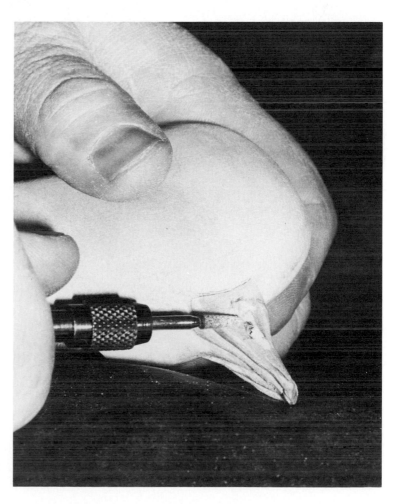

Grind very carefully around the nostril area, not just the hole but the entire area.

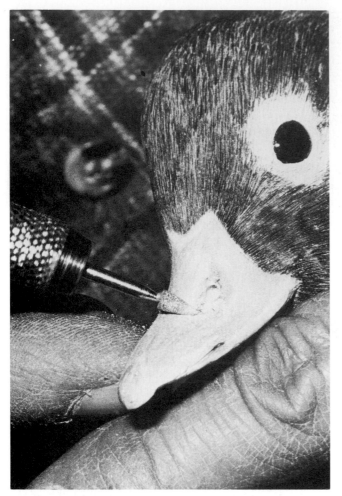

Carving upper ledge of nostril area.

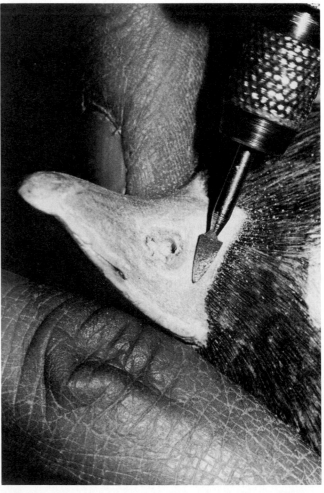

Smooth area around nostril with grinder. Note different bit. We are using a small tapered stone bit.

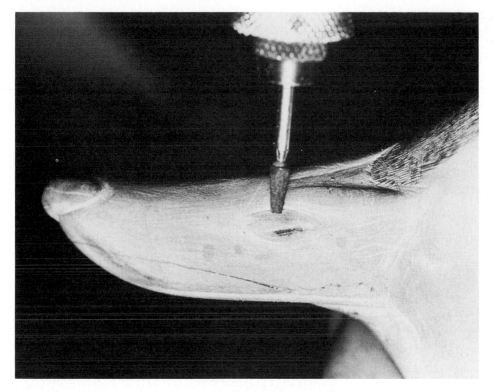

Touch up ledge over nostril.

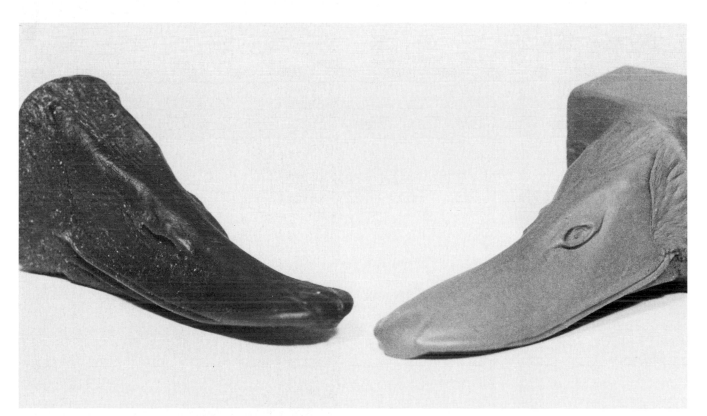

Canvasback bill (left) and mallard bill (right). Note difference between nostril shapes. Nostril area on canvasback sticks out like a ledge on top and is undercut on bottom. Mallard has a raised area around nostril hole; this area is pretty even all the way around.

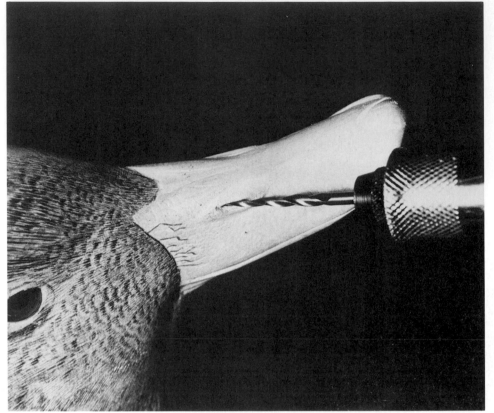

Now make the nostril hole by using a tapered carving drill. (You can also use a fine pointed knife or heat a nail and burn the hole in.)

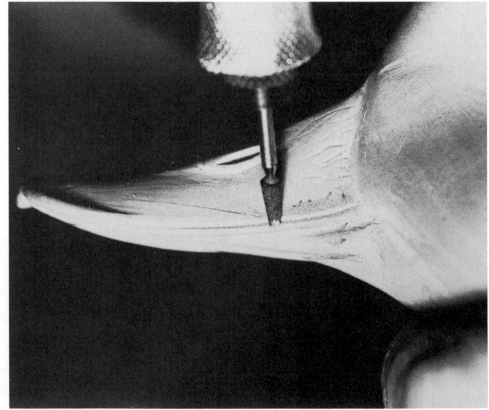

Time for finishing details—use grinder to carefully put in lip area on bill.

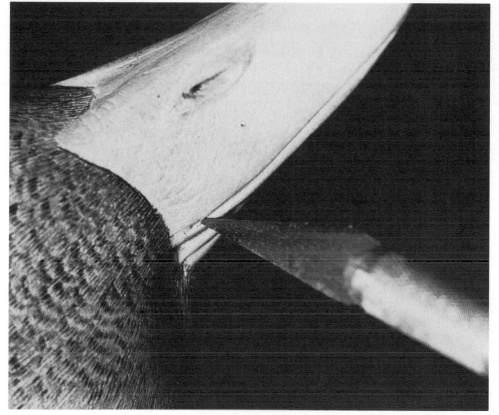

Xacto knife may be used instead of grinder to carve in lip area.

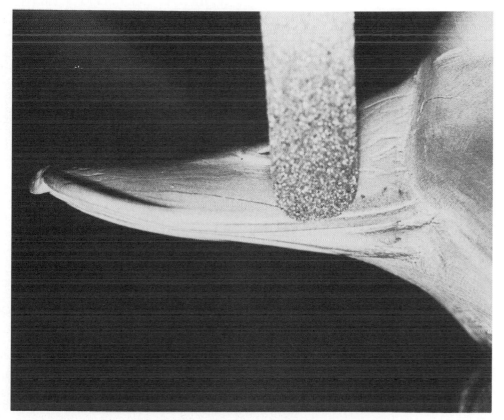

It is also possible to sand in lip area using a file or emery board.

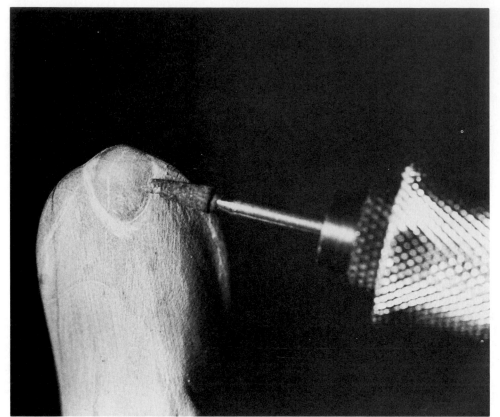

Carve in nail area using grinder and stone.

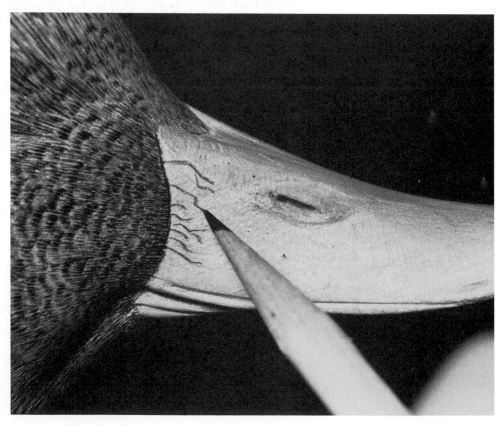

Draw in bill lines using a pencil or pen.

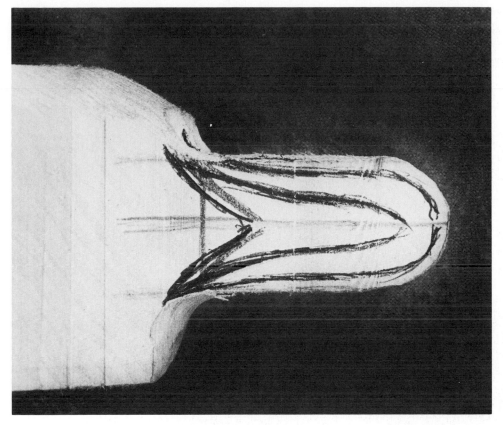

Lower mandible laid out for carving.

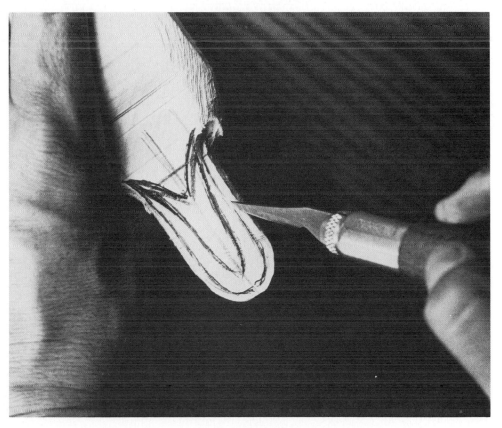

Cut from side of bill and roll over on to lower bill area with a knife.

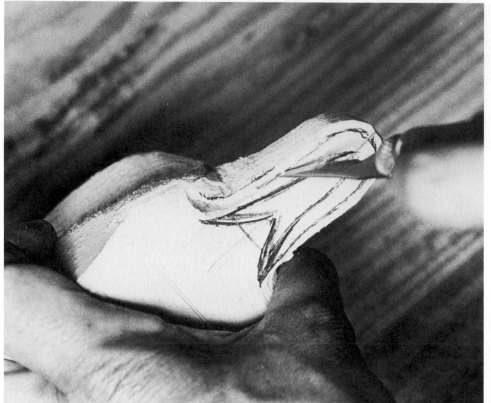

Continue cut on lower bill. Note knife is held with blade straight up and down on this cut.

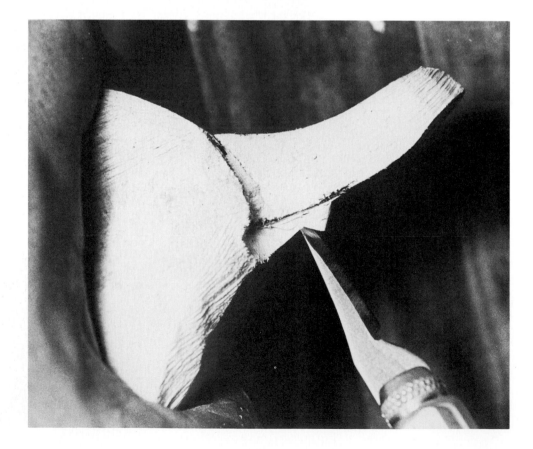

Recut side of bill

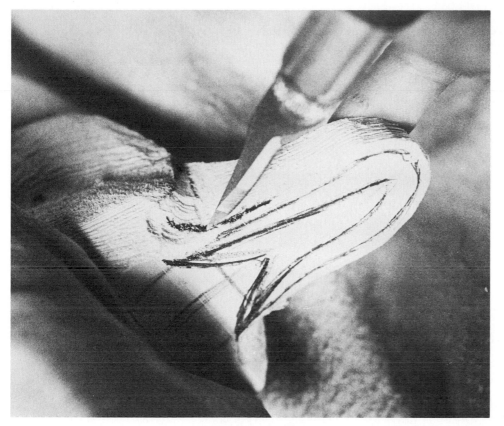

Roll the bill to cut on the bottom again.

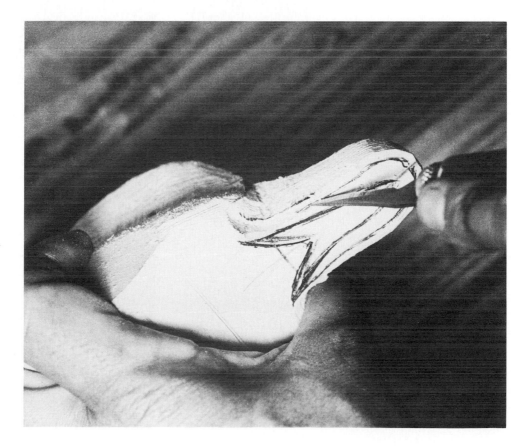

Clean out cut area.

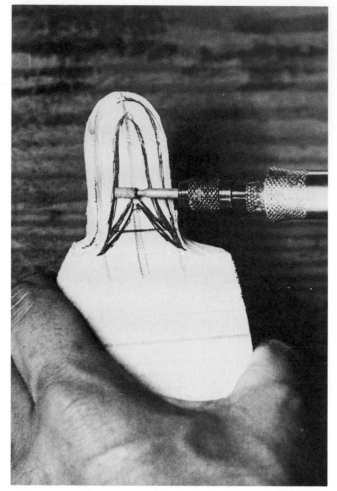

Using grinder with a cylinder stone instead of a knife.

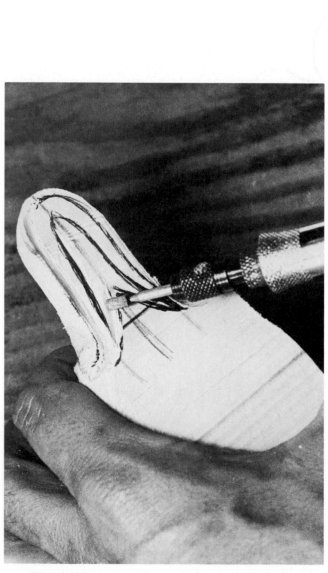

Carve chin area with a grinder and stone bit.

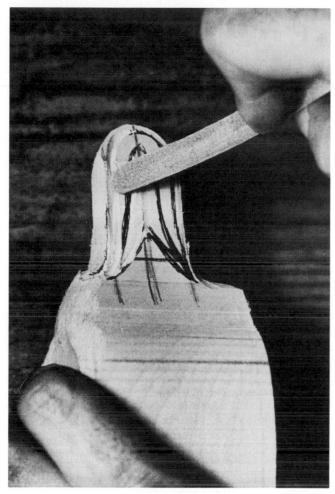

Clean cut area with a fingernail file.

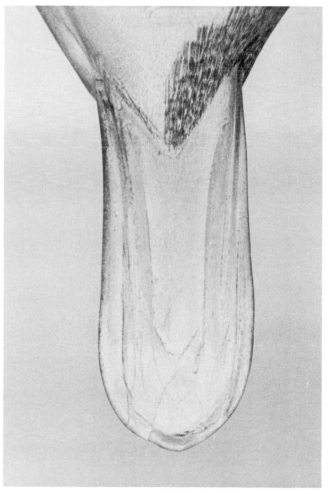

Lower mandible finished. Note chin area has been wood-burned to show how far chin feathers extend onto bill.

7

Carving the Body

Rough carving the body to its basic shape may be one of the easier tasks you do, once you understand the pattern or anatomical position you have chosen. Make sure you study your reference material very carefully before you attempt to carve the body shape.

It is important to understand where the bird's head and neck will be in relation to its shoulders. If you've chosen a relaxed, low-head position for your carving, the head and neck will be farther back than usual, perhaps as far as to rest between the shoulders. If you've chosen a drinking or swimming position, the head and neck will be farther ahead, or extended. With the head and neck extended other changes occur; for example, the cape feathers elongate and even stick up in the air in places. Sounds a little more complicated, but to make it easier we recommend a simple rule of thumb: Carve what you see, take time for the research.

Once you've carved the basic shape of the body, you'll master the technique of contouring, creating the flowing lines of the wildfowl. As always, knowledge of anatomy is vital, as you'll see when laying out the side pocket area, the group of feathers that cover the wings when they are folded against the body (sometimes called "ball feathers" by carvers). These feathers also act as insulation to retain body heat in cold weather. The front of the side pockets actually starts at the lower front area of the shoulders, or where the shoulders end. Depending on which species of duck or goose you have chosen, the side pocket area can be high or low. For instance, the teal group and some diving ducks, such as canvasbacks or redheads, have high side pocket areas. Other waterfowl such as the mallard are lower on the sides and look more level when viewed from the side. High and low here refer to the waterline in relation to the top of the back of the bird.

Enough said, let's get to work.

Great scaup with relaxed head. Note position of the neck and protruding breast area. You can also see the lumpy side pocket feathers.

Another low-head bird. This common goldeneye drake shows no neck at all. Head is back between shoulders and breast sticks out.

Mallard hen swimming forward. Head is semi-erect and starting to lean forward. Cape area shows behind neck.

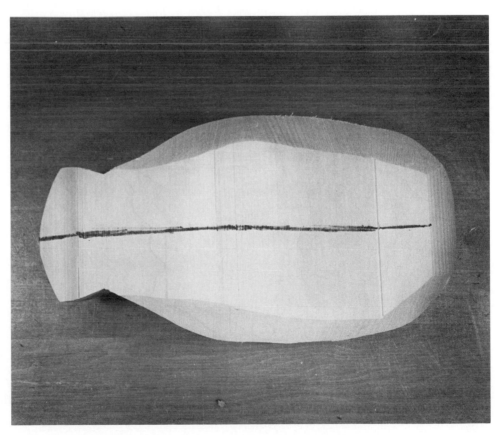

First step in rough carving the body: draw a center line down the top of the body.

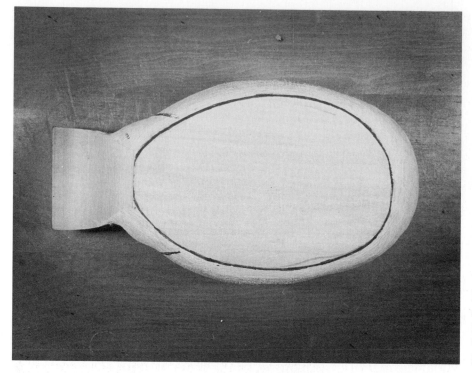

Turn wood block over and draw the bottom guideline: a continuous line around perimeter of the bottom of the body. This line should be ½ inch to ¾ inch in from outside edge of the bottom.

Start carving the body by rounding off all sharp corners until the bird is half round.

You can also use a file to round corners.

We use the grinder with large cone-shaped carbide cutter to round body. Round off the bottom up to guideline underneath the block. Round sides up to center line on the back.

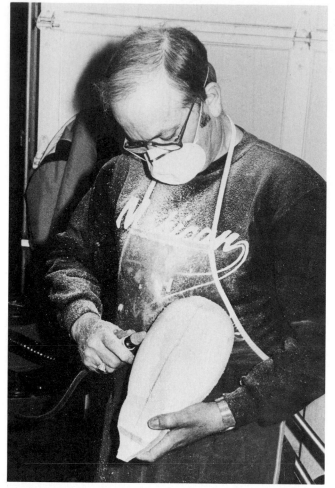

Body almost rounded. Note safety glasses and dust mask. An apron is also necessary. (The Michigan Tech sweatshirt is optional.)

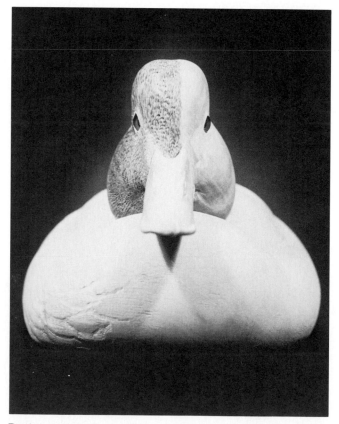

Body carved to desired round look (head temporarily attached).

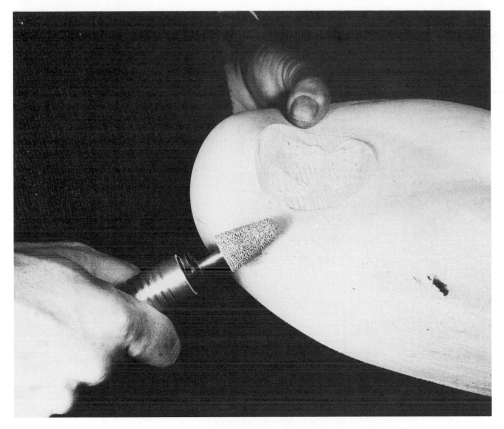

Carve in your shoulder areas. Assuming you have done your research and know where the shoulders are, start shaping by carving a trough on both sides of the head seat or the flat area where head will attach to body. (Use knife, file, draw knife, or grinder with ¾-inch cone-shaped carbide cutter.)

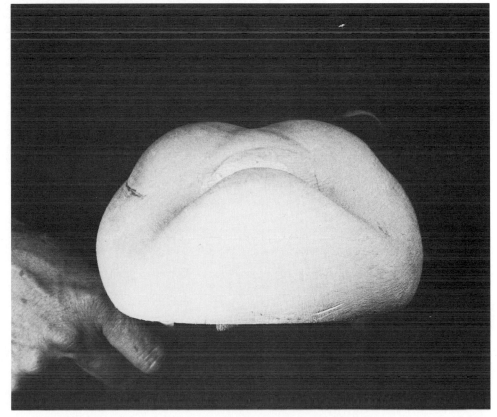

Neck trough on both sides. Note how trough changes front view of the bird, making it look like the breast area flows into the neck. (Note: When head and neck are back between shoulders, the breast area will be wider than that of a bird with head forward.)

With neck and shoulder area roughed out, temporarily attach head to body with a spot of glue from hot glue gun. (You can use a spot of any type glue. Just remember you will want to remove head again.) Once glue has dried, take grinder or knife and contour neck or base of head so that it flows into breast area.

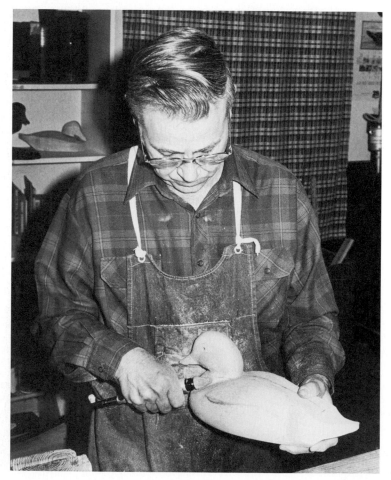

Carving neck area into a trough between shoulder and breast. Once more we bring up the word *research*. If you have done your research, you will know that the front of neck and sides flow evenly into breast area that sticks out.

A sanding drum can also be used for contouring.

Body rounded with head in place and neck area done. Note flow from neck onto breast area.

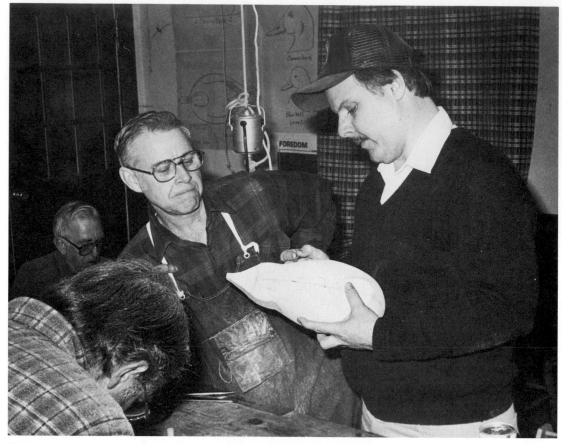

Next step is to lay out side pocket area. Here, Clark Sullivan (on right) shows students side pocket area prior to laying out the lines.

Draw side pocket lines, starting at the front near trough area you carved in the block. In most cases, side pocket guideline from side view will be lower near shoulder area, swoop upward to cover wings, then back down near end of pocket where feet and legs stick out.

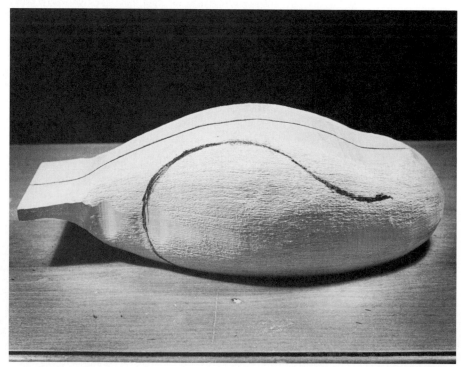

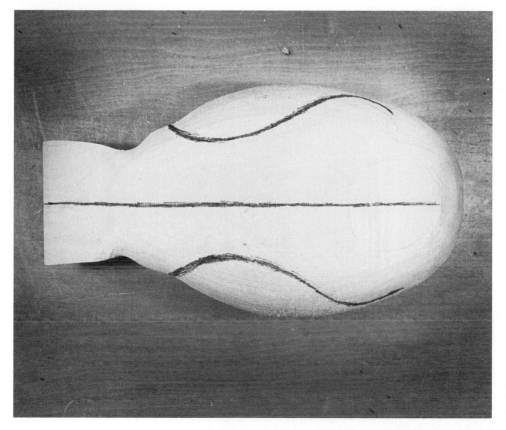

Look at block from the top to make sure lines look equal distance from your center line on the back.

Also check body from the front. Starting point of side pocket lines on each side of neck should be same distance up from bottom of block.

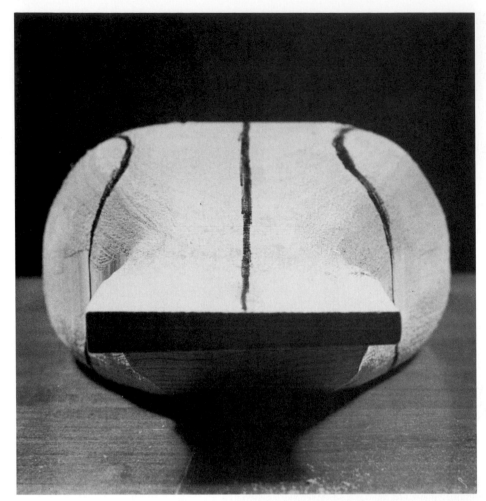

Final check—the rear view—to insure that lines are even.

Start carving side pocket area with ¾-inch cone-shaped carbide cutter (V gouge or round chisel may also be used). Method is similar to carving eye channel area—carve a channel along the line and clean it out along top and bottom. Cut this area again and reclean trough area. This channel should be cut about ½ inch to ¾ inch depending on the species. Remember these are feather groups covering other feather groups, so do not leave a deep channel or trough.

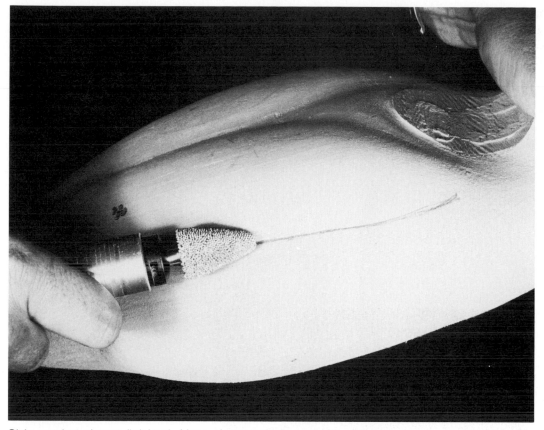

Side pocket almost finished. Note clean trough area. No ridges or gouges show, just an indented area along the line. Smooth out everything to a nice flow from one group to another.

Next, check your reference material and measure if possible, or gauge as close as you can, the cape area, the V-shaped group of feathers behind the neck. These feathers are topmost layer on back and cover over shoulder area. You can actually go around edge of cape feather area and lift outside edge of feathers. Draw in lines and start carving with gouge or carbide cutter.

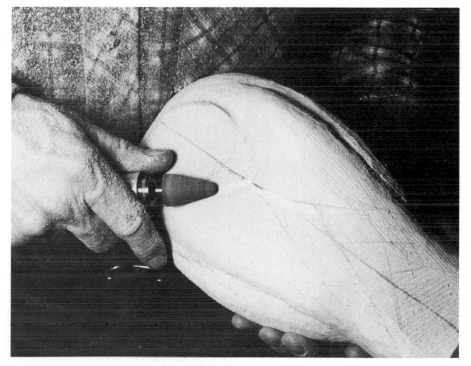

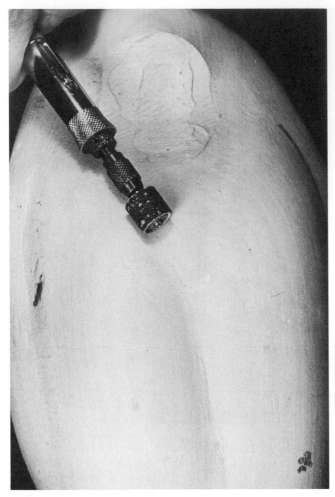

Finishing cape area with sanding drum. Cape will be recessed in the middle and slightly higher at outside edge because feathers are highest in build-up at that point.

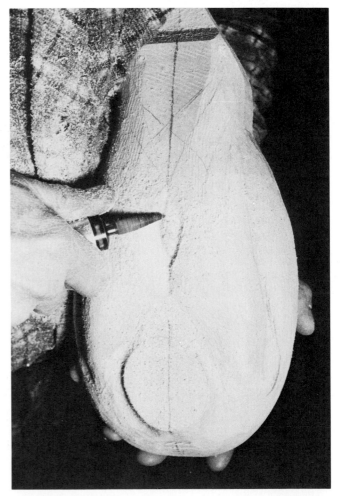

At the back or point of cape, wings are joined together and there will be a trough area between wings in most cases. Trough may appear more predominant or less depending on the attitude of the bird. It should be like a valley, rounded off on top edges and at the bottom. This area is tricky, so make sure you look hard at feather configuration where wings join in middle of the back before you start carving.

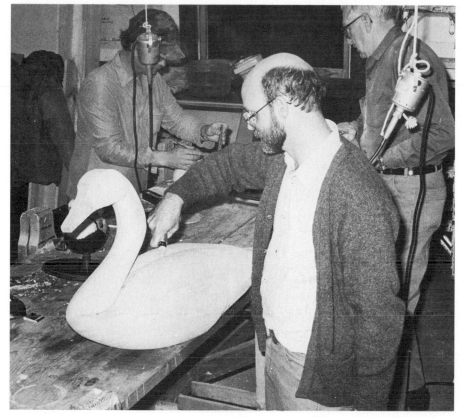

The trough ends about two-thirds of the way from breast to tail. It's best to measure from tip of tail (if you have a mount) up to point where trough splays out. The depth of the trough will vary on almost every specie depending on the position of the waterfowl.

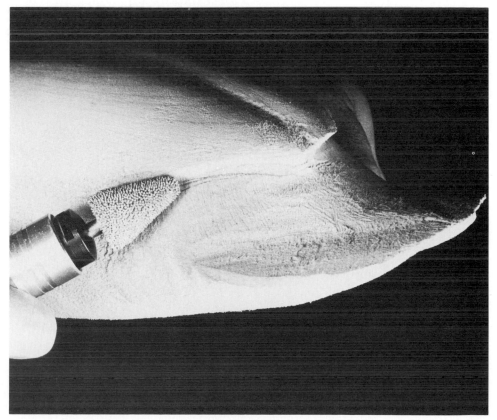

Raised tertial area above tail. The wood on both sides of trough should be left as high as possible since it will be the stock from which you will carve tertial feathers (more on this later).

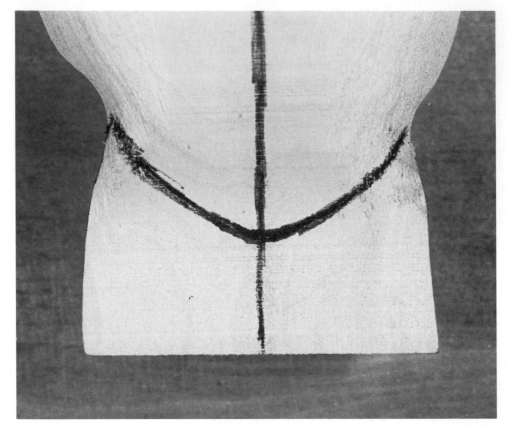

Next area to lay out and carve is the tail (top view and rump area pictured). If you are carving a tail with feathers spread apart (open tail) or a closed tail, you should be able to determine length of tail feathers from tip to upper tail coverts (feathers). Place a mark at the point and another on each side of tail where feathers start out of the body. Draw a semicircle to middle around to other side.

Draw same lines underneath tail. Be careful—feathers underneath sometimes go farther towards end of tail than do top feathers.

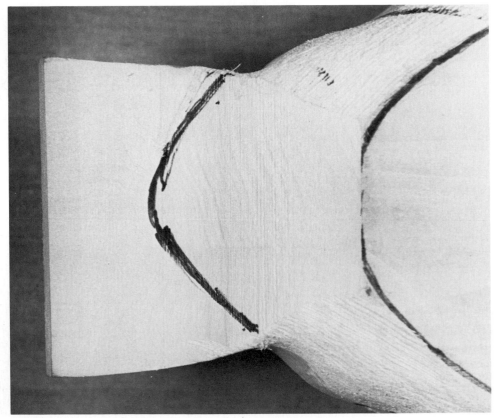

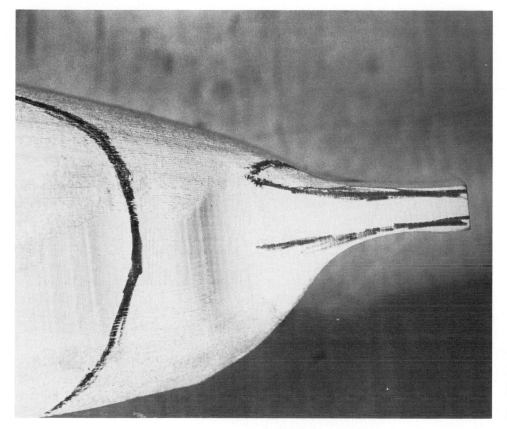

Draw two more guidelines, one on each side of tail on edge to allow sufficient thickness (3/8 inch) to carve each feather. Now you are ready to start carving upper and lower tail areas.

Start carving a trough around base of the tail where it comes out of the body with cone-shaped cutter. This trough will be deeper near sides of tail because tail tends to slant downward to base. (Degree of slant differs from divers to dabblers and even from one attitude to another of the same bird.)

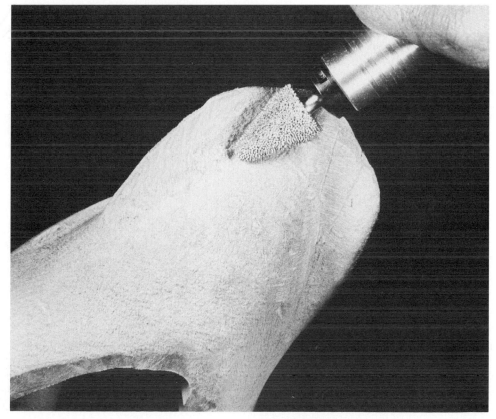

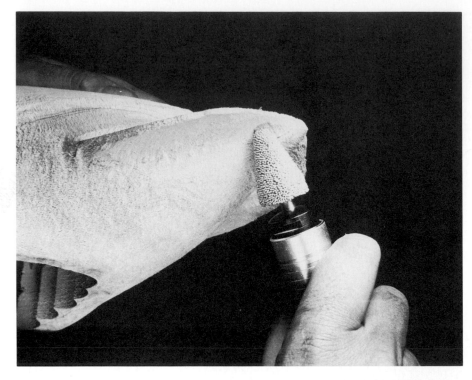

Leave area in center of tail near base the highest because upper tail coverts flow down on top of tail feathers. Rest of tail section is carved evenly on sides and high in middle to give tent-shaped appearance when viewed from back.

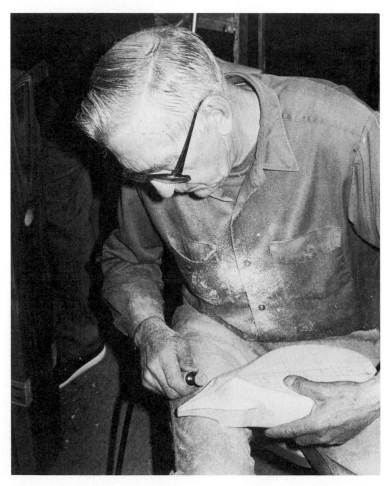

Use ball-shaped cutter to carve bottom just the reverse, with outside edges high and center low. One exception: leave rump area high in center. (If you are carving a mallard drake and wondering about curl feathers on top, we suggest these be carved separately and inserted later when tail has been completely carved.)

8

Feather Groups

It is important to know and understand the different feather groups before you begin to carve them. Rather than describe and show the feather groups for every species of waterfowl, we will concentrate on the anatomical basics. We trust you'll make a careful study of the particular species you've chosen to carve.

First, realize that the feather groups are the same for ducks and geese. The feathers of diving ducks, however, differ in shape and length from those of dabbling ducks. The major difference appears to be in the shape of the tertial feathers and primary feathers. Dabbling ducks have longer wings, so the primary feathers, or flight feathers, stick out farther from beneath the tertial feathers. Their tertial feathers also tend to be full in shape, in contrast to the long and pointed shape of tertials on the diving ducks.

Feather direction is the same for all waterfowl. All feathers flow from the head to the tail, overlapping like shingles or scales. Pro-

ceeding in this direction, let's start with the group of feathers on the top of the head, the crown feathers. These are followed by the neck feathers, which appear more like hairs than feathers. Next come the breast feathers in front of the neck and the cape area behind the neck. These are followed by the side pocket feather group on the sides, or flanks, and the scapulars on the back and shoulder feathers, or coverts. Underneath are the belly feathers, which you will not be concerned with unless you carve a full-bodied bird. Next come the longer, tertial feathers on the back, right behind the scapular feathers. On the sides of the tail and above and below the tail are more coverts, aptly named the upper, lower, and side tail coverts. The feathers right under the tertial feathers, in the middle of the back just over the upper tail coverts, are the oil gland coverts.

The wing feathers are broken into several groups of feathers situated on the upper surface of the wing, on the bottom, and under-

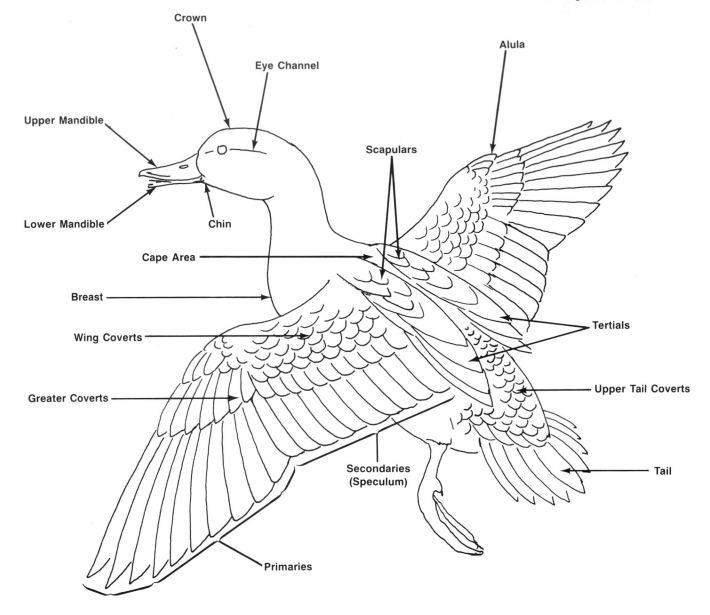

neath the wing. Let's concentrate on the groups you should know for the basic carving. The first group, and the most obvious, are the long, slender flight feathers, or primaries. These are the feathers you will see crossed over the rump area of the bird. They extend from under the tertial feathers down over the rump.

Diver wings, being shorter than dabblers', may go just to the edge of the tail or just short of the tail. The diver primaries also tend to lie down flatter on the rump. Dabbler primaries sometimes cross and extend over the tail area; they also tend to stick up in the air higher than diver primaries.

The next group, which usually are the colorful feathers on the wing, are called the secondaries. These feathers are stacked just below the primaries and come out of the side pocket near the end of the pocket. In some cases, depending on the attitude of the bird, these feathers show very little or not at all.

Take the time to learn these feather groups; study their various shapes and sizes and closely examine the direction of flow. Your research will certainly enhance the final look of your bird.

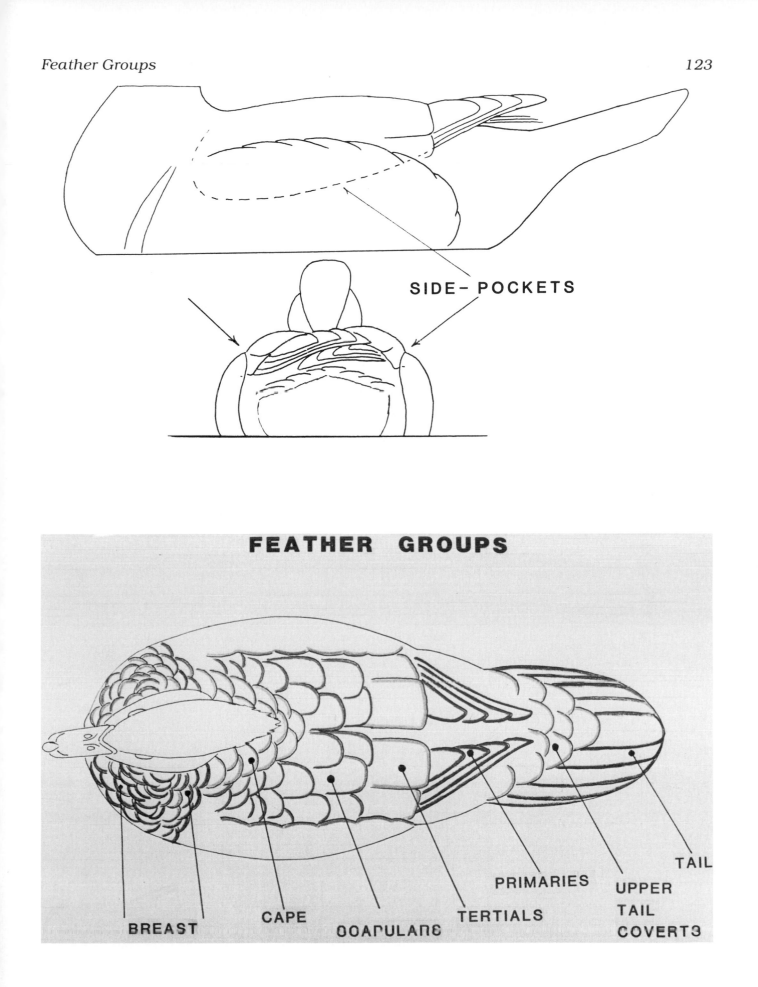

SIDE-POCKETS

FEATHER GROUPS

BREAST

CAPE

SCAPULARS

TERTIALS

PRIMARIES

UPPER TAIL COVERTS

TAIL

Redhead hen (diver) on left, widgeon hen (dabbler) on right. Note difference in length and shape of feathers.

Arrows show direction and flow of feathers. (Cinnamon teal pictured.)

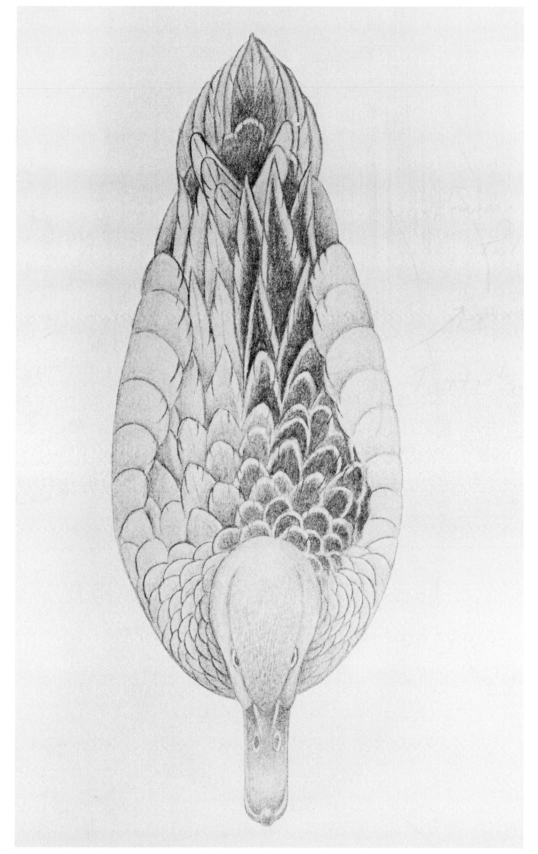

Top view showing the feather groups. Note the direction of these feathers. (Cinnamon teal pictured.)

Good top view of a gadwall drake. Note more pointed feathers.

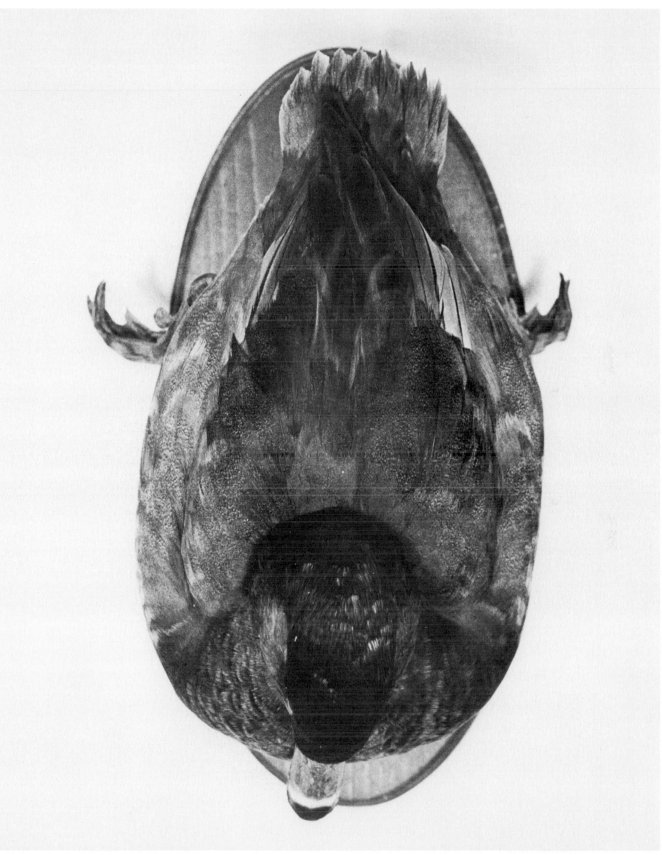

Good top view of a redhead hen. Note more rounded feathers.

Side profile of a green-winged teal drake. Note the tertials and primaries. The scapulars stick up over the tertials. Note cone shape or tent shape of scapulars and tertials.

Basic Color Theory

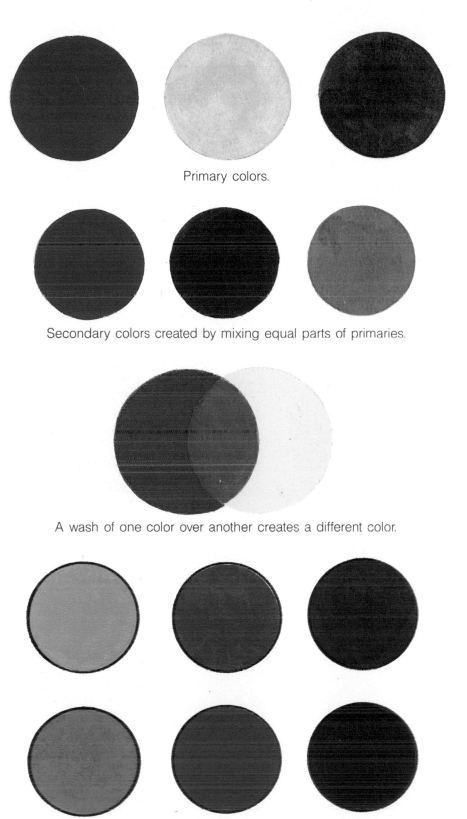

Primary colors.

Secondary colors created by mixing equal parts of primaries.

A wash of one color over another creates a different color.

Intermediate colors created by adding more or less of a primary color to a secondary color.

The three values of black: dark, medium, and light.

The three values of white: dark, medium, and light.

Practice technique for smooth blending. Determine where your light source is coming from and blend from this area all the way through to darkest-shaded area.

Practicing washes, on paper, will give you an idea of how much water to mix with the paint to create a workable wash.

Painting the Heads of a Drake Woodduck and Hen Mallard— A Procedure Applicable to Carvings of Other Species

Step One: Determine base colors—green on the woodduck (left) and a light brown (sienna) or ochre on the mallard (right).

Step Two: Simulate highlights (light areas) and shadows (dark areas) of the live bird. On woodduck use yellow, Hooker's green, and thalo green. On mallard use yellow ochre, white, and raw umber. Use thin washes; otherwise, you'll fill in your textured lines and paint will take on a hard gloss. (We've also started to lay down the dark streaks on the mallard.)

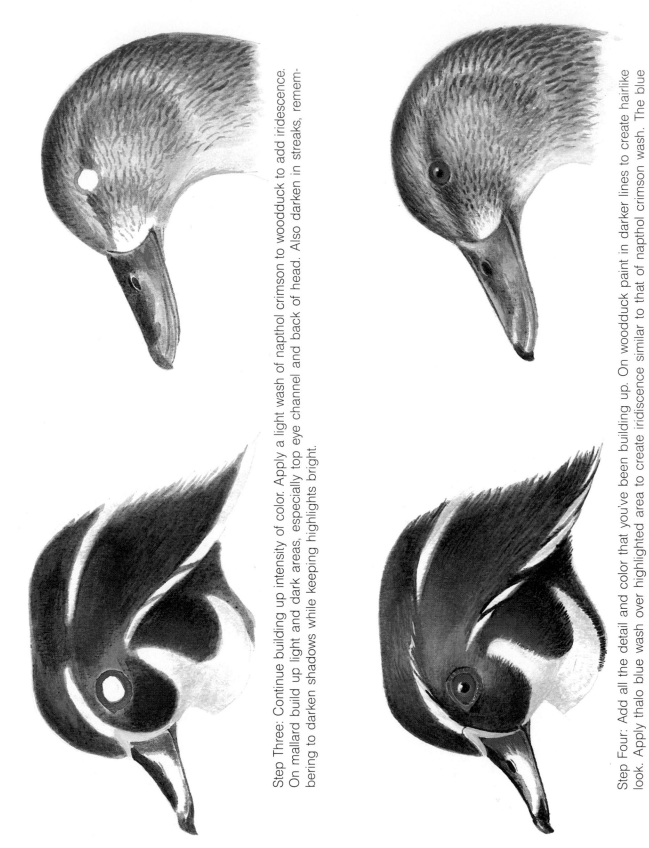

Step Three: Continue building up intensity of color. Apply a light wash of napthol crimson to woodduck to add iridescence. On mallard build up light and dark areas, especially top eye channel and back of head. Also darken in streaks, remembering to darken shadows while keeping highlights bright.

Step Four: Add all the detail and color that you've been building up. On woodduck paint in darker lines to create hairlike look. Apply thalo blue wash over highlighted area to create iridiscence similar to that of napthol crimson wash. The blue transforms crimson to purplish color and the green to blue-green. (It is imperative that you experiment since numerous shades are possible.) On mallard, highlight and shade to finished stage by applying washes of yellow ochre and white. Continue accenting specific areas to create illusion of light and dark.

Painting Iridescence on a Drake Bufflehead

Areas to show iridescence are blocked out by using washes of napthol crimson and white for pinkish color, and napthol crimson and cadmium yellow light for yellow-orange color.

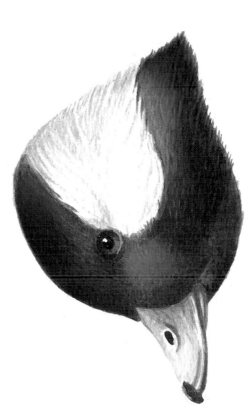

Step Four: By working the various washes around, you can create a more intense iridescence. A wash of thalo blue over the red creates a violet to purple iridescence.

Step One: Apply basic green base, with accents on highlights and shadows, using Hooker's green, cadmium yellow light, and thalo blue.

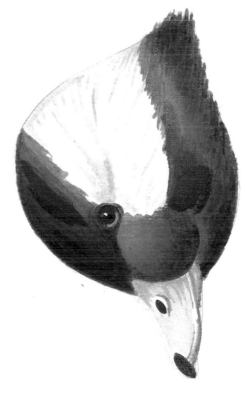

Step Three: Washes of thalo blue over different areas provide a blue-green when washed over the yellow-green, and a dark blue-green over the Hooker's green.

Detail Work

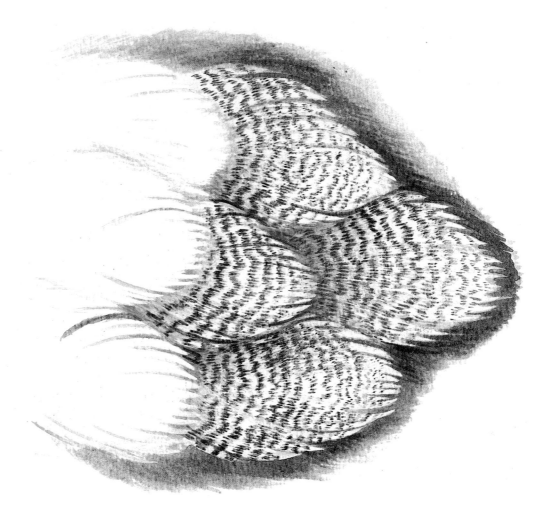

Vermiculation—the wavy bands or lines on feathers—can vary in lightness and darkness.

Painting with the three values of black (left) enables you to create an illusion of feather edges. Use the three values of white (right) to paint feathers and create the illusion of depth.

Note the variations of color on the bills of a drake mallard (left) and drake canvasback (right). Re-create highlights and shadows on areas such as top of bill, lip, and nostril, and lower mandible.

Putting it all together—soft, complementary colors and markings on a drake lesser scaup.

Live Birds

Mandarin duck drake.

Lesser scaup hen.

Bluc winged teal drake.

Canvasback drake.

Gadwall drake.

Gadwall hen.

Canvasback hen.

Buttlehead drake

Canvasback hen and drake

Common goldeneye.

Common goldeneye.

Snow goose.

Canada goose.

Blue goose.

Hen ringneck.

White-fronted goose.

Redhead drake.

Old squaw drake.

Woodduck drake.

Ringneck drake.

Green-winged teal drake.

Barrows goldeneye drake.

Whistling swan.

Whistling swan.

Mounted Specimens

Old squaw drake.

Hooded merganser drake.

Redhead hen.

Harlequin drake. (From the collection of Chuck and Carol Hilts)

Bufflehead drake. (From the collection of Chuck and Carol Hilts)

Head detail of common goldeneye drake.

Head detail of bufflehead drake.

Decorative Carvings

Ruddy—Dale Dinse, Flushing, Michigan.
(1984 Best of Show Novice Division, Ward
Foundation World Championships)

Black Duck—Russ Brannon, Flint, Michigan.

Ringneck—Erwin Pillsbury, Flint, Michigan. (1984 Best of Show Amateur Division, California; 1984 First Place Professional Division, Midwest Decoy Contest; 1984 First Place Amateur Division, Ward Foundation World Championships)

Widgeon—Dick Corr, Lansing, Michigan. (1984 First Place Novice Division, Ward Foundation World Championships)

Whistling Swan—Carl Chapell, Fenton, Michigan. (1981 Best of Show Amateur Division, Ward Foundation World Championships)

Old Squaw—Clark Sullivan, Swartz Creek, Michigan.

Bufflehead—Howard Nixon, Chesaning, Michigan. (1985 First Place Toronto Sportsman Show)

Shoveler—Clark Sullivan, Swartz Creek, Michigan.

9

Laying Out the Feathers

Now that you have a better understanding of the feather groups, it will be easier to measure and lay them out for carving. The first step will require taking some measurements with the calipers. Make sure your carving has a center line for reference before you start laying out your feathers. Whether you start at the front of the bird or the tail, you should take some time to measure the feathers group by group, feather by feather. We start with the tail area by measuring from a photograph of the top view of the bird blown up to life-size or from a study mount. Use caution when measuring from a mounted specimen; you are at the mercy of the taxidermist and can not make the assumption that his or her work is correct. It boils down to that familiar word, research.

There's a temptation to start carving once you've laid out a particular group of feathers, say, the tail feathers. You can do this, but you should be aware of the possibility that the rest of the feathers on the back and cape area may not fit in where they belong. It pays to check the measurements all the way up to the cape area. We prefer to lay out *all* the feathers and draw in the shafts, and even the splits you see in the feathers. This method tends to bring the carving together.

There is no set pattern in laying out your bird's feathers. Start where you like when you have reached a point where you feel at ease. We usually start with the tertial feathers and work up to the cape area. We usually do the tail last.

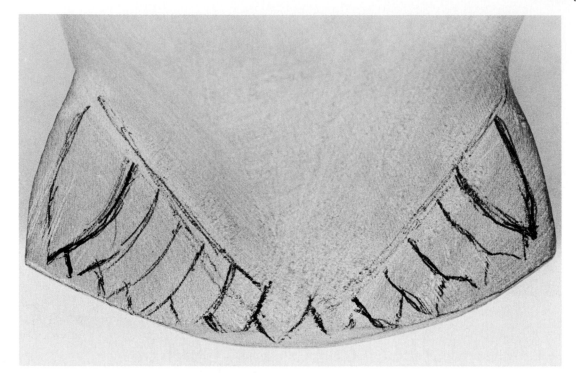

First measure length and width of lower tail feathers. Draw them on block of wood, making sure you notice direction of feathers and which feather is on top. Tail feathers are stacked in a down-stairs pattern, with one or two center feathers being the top stair.

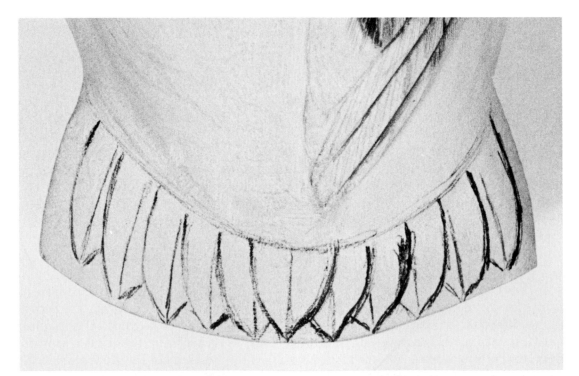

Lay out upper tail feathers (this carving shows only one center feather). Note direction of stacking is reverse that of lower-tail-feather stacking. It helps to draw the shafts of feathers to see the flow.

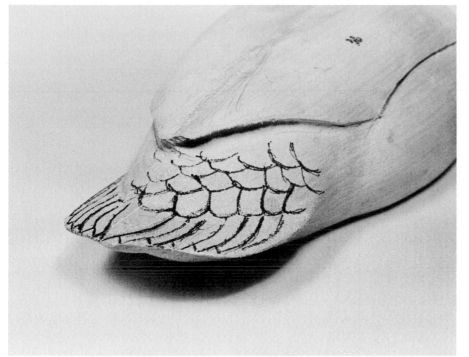

Next group to lay out: upper tail coverts. If you like, lay out side and lower tail coverts at this time also. These feathers seem to be pretty much the same shape on most birds in the waterfowl group. Some may be rounder on the edges or more pointed, so look closely. Check for length and width also—making these too skinny, fat, or long will be apparent to professional carvers and judges.

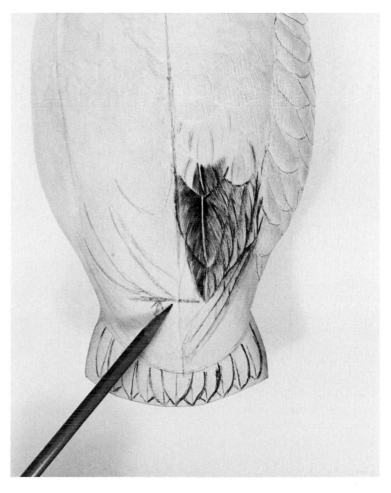

Now lay out tertial feathers, the long feathers that lie on top of primary feathers. Check reference material for (1) side profile to get a feel for how tertials come out of upper rear area of side pocket feathers; (2) top view to see how tertials follow direction of primaries. Measure from tip of tail to back tip of tertials and place a mark on the wood. Draw a line across block for back edge. (If you've designed your bird properly, you'll have a higher area cut out for tertials.) Measure length and width of tertials one at a time and draw them in. Notice tertials will cross over center line if wings are to be crossed. (We bypass primaries for now, since we prefer to carve them separately and insert them. See chapter 10.)

Lay out scapular feathers. They're longer near tertials and shorter up near cape area. You can measure these from where you left off on tertials. Note scapulars have different shape than tertials.

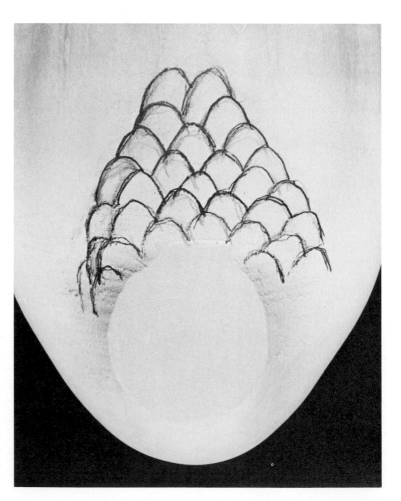

Last group on the back: the cape feather group, which forms cape-like area behind head of bird. Note directions of cape feathers around base of neck, especially near sides of neck. Cape feathers in this area actually cover over shoulder feathers and slant more toward the back than downward. Easiest mistake is to make them too small; in most cases, these feathers will be about the size of a dime near the end of each feather. Actually they would be almost shaped like half of a dime. This is only approximation of size and shape, so check these feathers on your reference material very carefully.

With all back feathers laid out, next group is breast feathers. Also shaped like half of a dime up near neck, they get slightly larger as they flow down and back and merge with side pocket feathers. Transformation from breast feathers to side pocket feathers is done by a *gradual* increase in size. (Common mistake is to draw breast feathers all the same size and then draw large side pocket feathers.) Note also direction: at front of neck and breast, breast feathers go straight down center; moving toward sides, they splay out toward side and back.

Last group to lay out: side pocket feathers, and that is exactly what they are, a pocket. They cover the wings, acting as insulation to retain body heat. Here, wing is starting to fold into side pocket. Note primary feathers folding under secondaries.

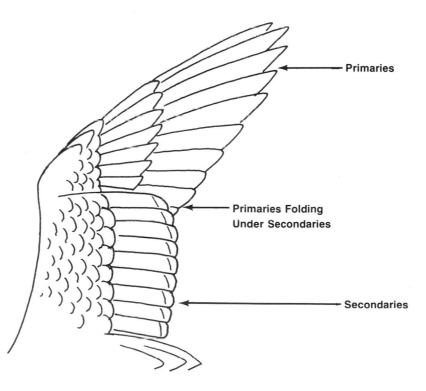

Primaries

Primaries Folding
Under Secondaries

Secondaries

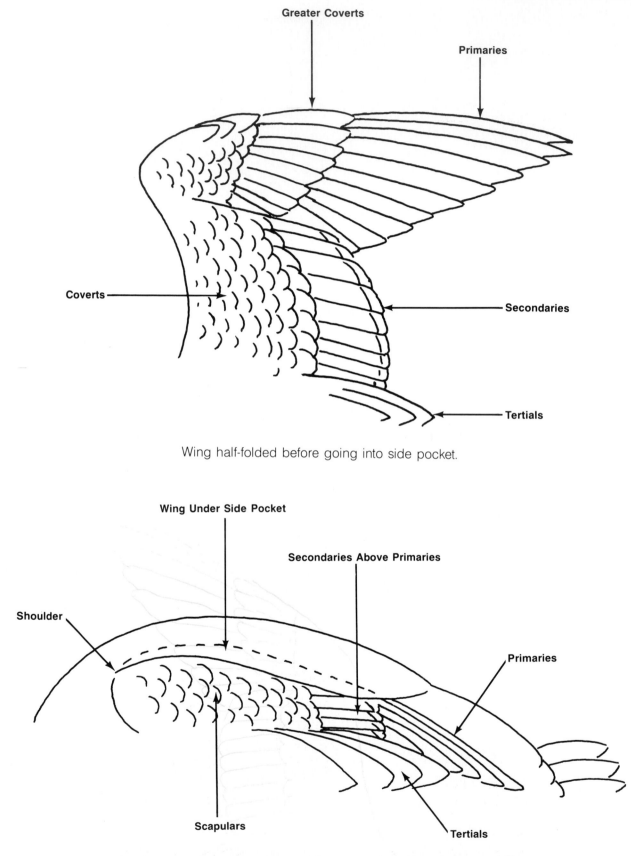

Wing half-folded before going into side pocket.

Wing folded all the way into the side pocket area. Note feather stacking.

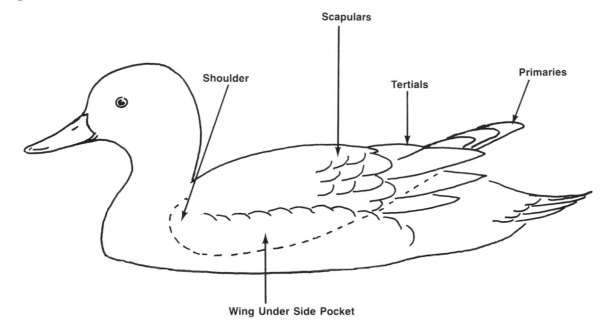

Side view of wing in side pocket.

On hot summer days you will see waterfowl, such as this pintail drake, with wings spread apart and hanging down on sides—perhaps their way of releasing body heat to cool off.

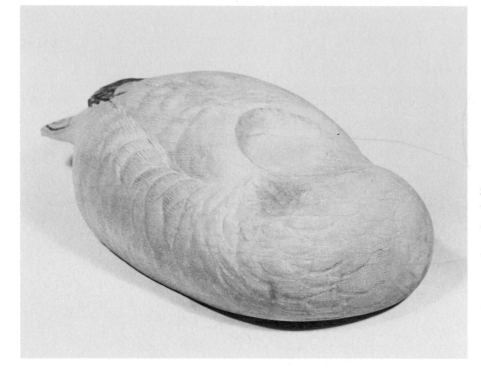

Side pocket feathers get larger towards the rear and their flow is back and up. Top row of feathers covers part of the back area, flowing upward and over shoulders and scapulars and even part of tertials. Top row is actually a row, changing from smaller to larger feathers. Study side pocket feathers and do the necessary measuring before laying them out.

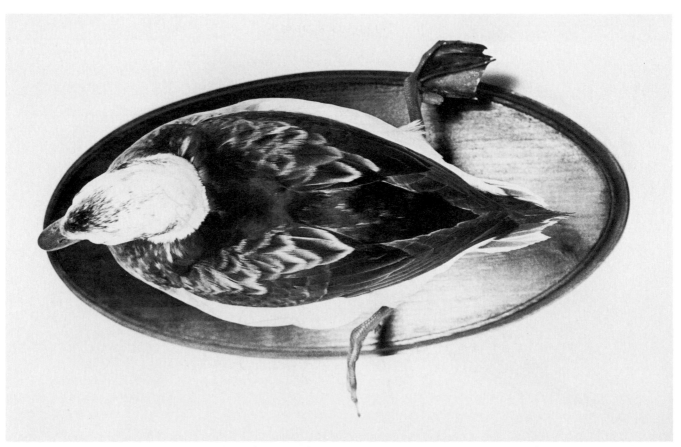

Old squaw hen. Note the shape and flow of the feathers. Primary feathers are long for a diving duck.

Ruddy duck drake.

Common goldeneye hen. Primaries are long.

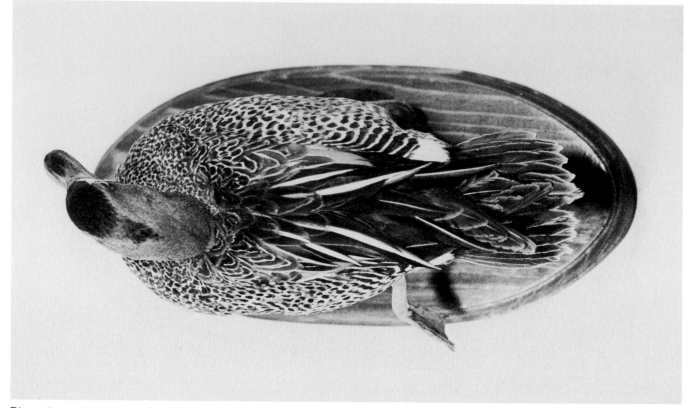

Blue-winged teal drake. Side pocket feathers are way up on back area. After carving several waterfowl, you'll become adept enough to accurately draw these feathers freehand.

10

Carving the Feathers

Once the feather groups are laid out, you can start carving one group at a time. We usually start with the tertials, since these are the rearmost feathers that cover the primaries and seem to carry the flow of the feathers on the back. We spoke earlier of the ridge, or excess height, we leave on the back for the tertials. This extra height can be up to an inch or more on some dabbling ducks because their primaries and tertials tend to stick up higher than those of diving ducks. Take time in your research to notice how high the tertials and primaries can stick up on the teal family and the widgeon, for instance. Viewed from the rear, the tertials of a dabbling duck are also apt to have a greater cone shape, or tented effect, than do the tertials of a diving duck. Be sure to study this feather group before carving.

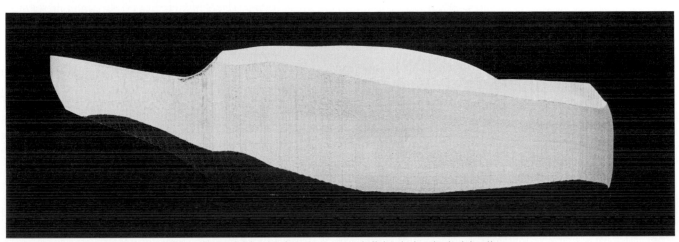

Side view of block showing area left high for tertial feathers.

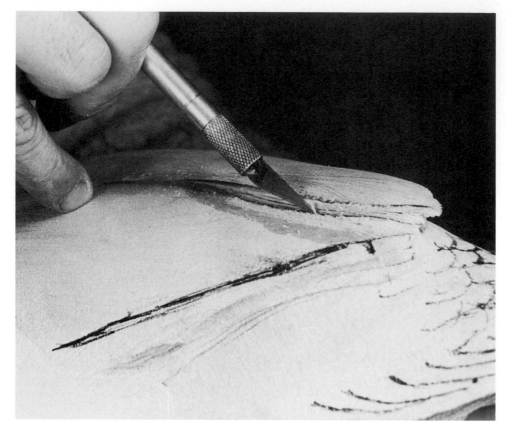

You can start carving tertials with Xacto knife, or any knife for that matter. With Xacto knife, we feel we have more control and are able to cut clean edges. You'll have to cut down into wood a lot farther than you think, sometimes up to half an inch or more around tertials. Remember, tertials are on top of primaries, ends held up in the air by primaries. Cut accordingly.

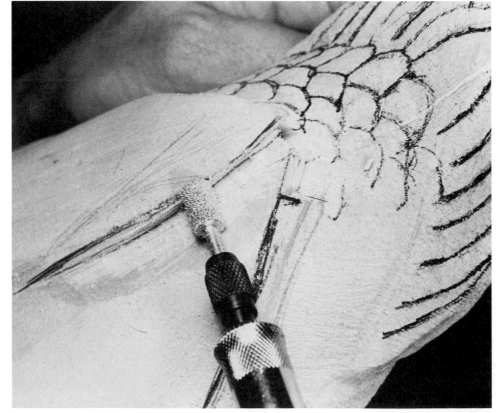

We grind tertials on outside edge and then go to Xacto knife.

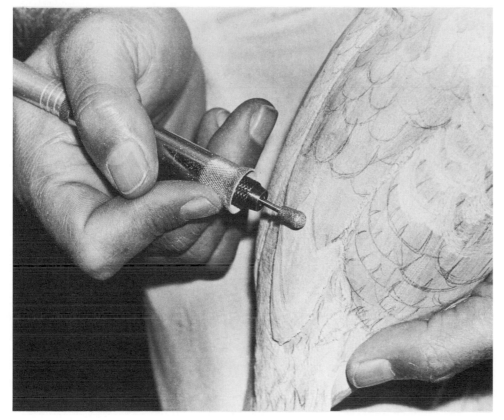

Use ruby carver to outline each feather. Regardless of the tool you use, we find it better to outline each feather before you finish carving each feather.

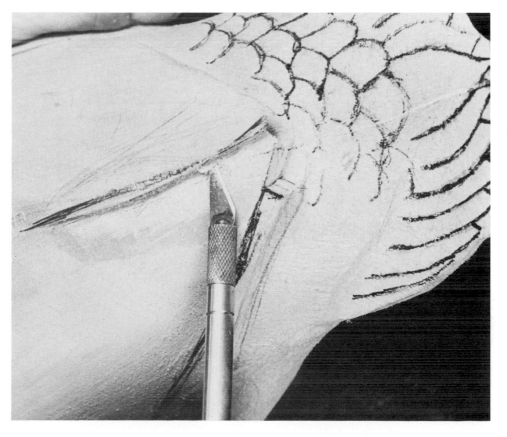

After tertials are rough-cut, go ahead and bevel edges down so feathers are tent-shaped. Undercut tertials so primaries can slide underneath.

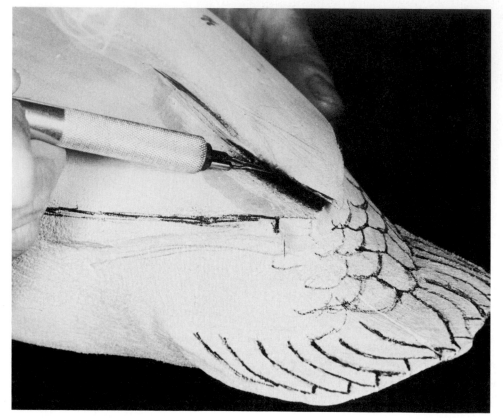

Undercutting using a wood burner.

Side view of tertials cut. Note how high they are.

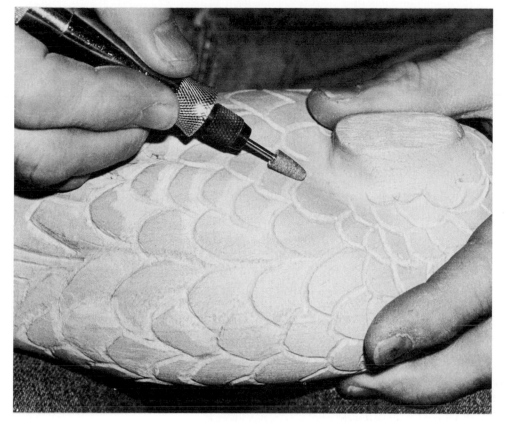

Now carve scapulars. We prefer a flexible shaft tool with ruby carver point. (You can also use Xacto knife or chisel with U-shaped blade. Whatever tool you use, remember that no raised edges should show—real feathers are not like fish scales.) Shape feathers by tapering them toward rear of feather. Blend one into the other with a nice flow, sanding off all edges.

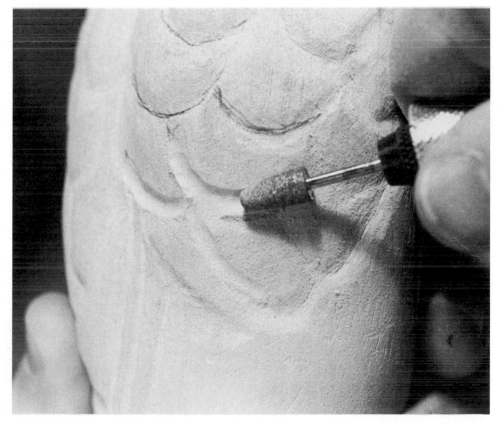

Use same technique—outlining then blending—for side pocket feathers (pictured here), cape and breast feathers, and tail coverts.

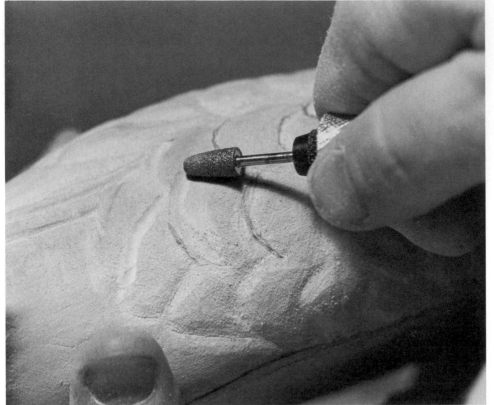

Smoothing feather edges with ruby carver will make texturing a lot more simple later on.

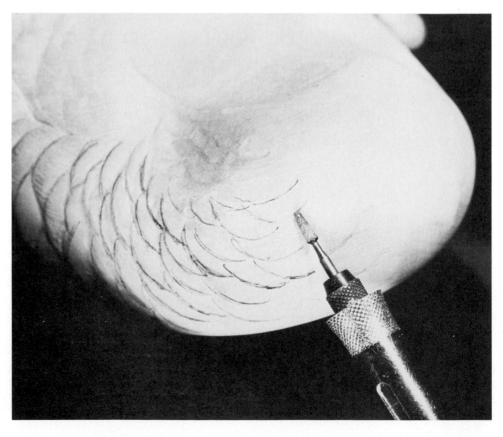

Grinding breast feathers with a stone or ruby carver. Smooth edges down also.

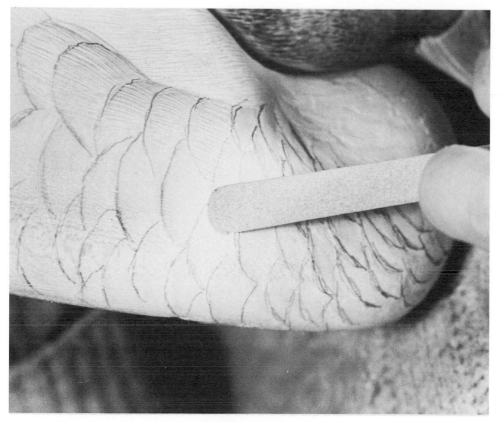

Polish edges with fingernail file or sandpaper.

Cut tail feathers with Xacto knife (cylinder-shaped ruby carver or stone may also be used). Whenever you use a knife you risk leaving a knife-cut mark which sometimes is difficult to hide, so cut lightly.

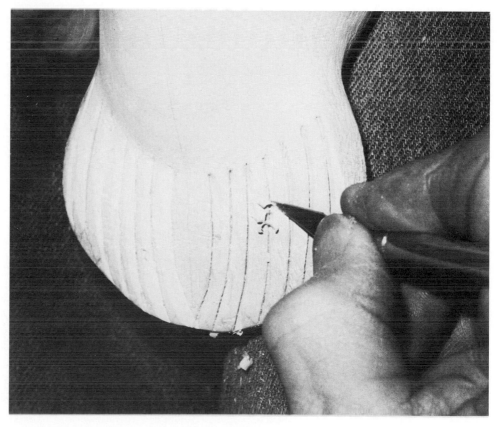

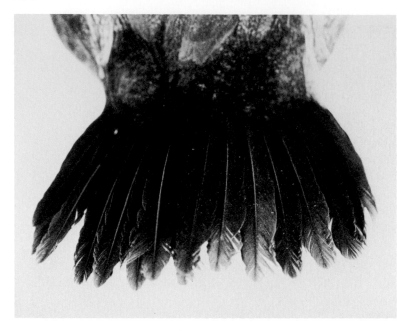

Good top view of tail feathers. Note detail of feathers and how they are stacked. This fanned-out tail is similar to the one we are carving.

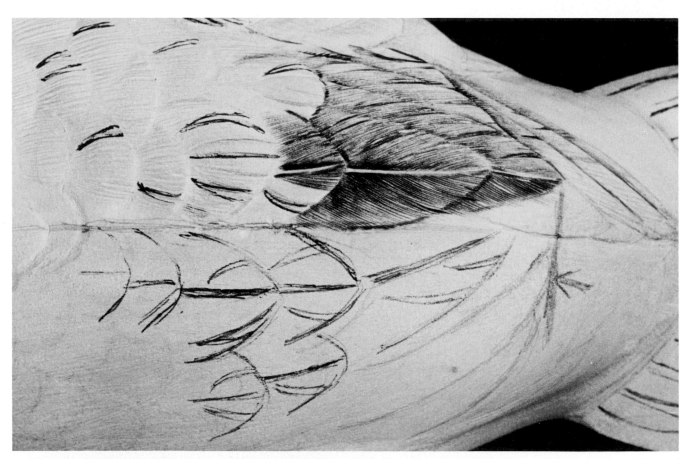

Once all feathers are carved and sanded, lay out splits and shafts with pencil. Note that splits start near shaft and follow contour of feather. Some birds appear neater than others, so don't go overboard with the splits. Shafts are visible on tail feathers, tertials, and some scapulars. They are not visible on cape, head, breast, side pockets, or coverts, so do not draw or carve them in.

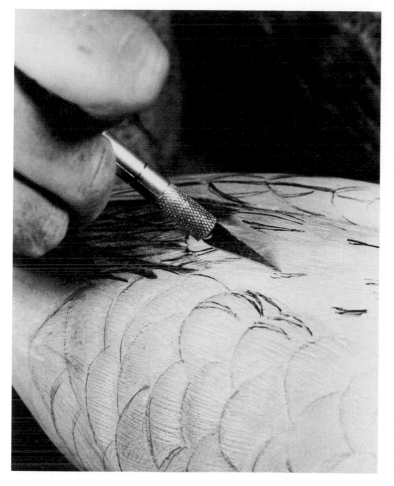

Splits and shafts can be cut in with Xacto knife. Cut on each side of split on an angle and clean out wood. On shaft, cut lightly on each side and plane wood away very carefully.

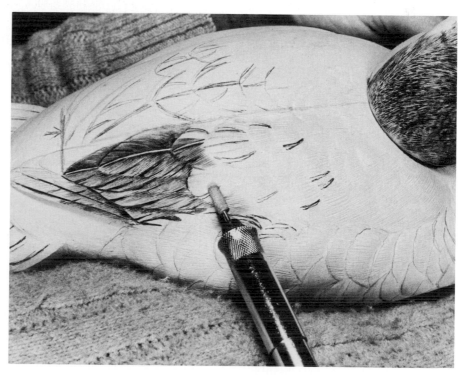

You can get same effect with cylinder-shaped stone, using its edge to cut splits.

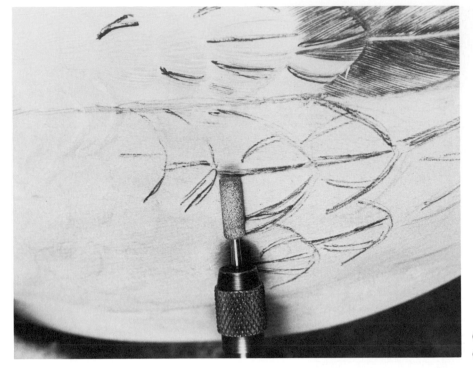

On shafts, run stone down both sides of shaft to relieve wood.

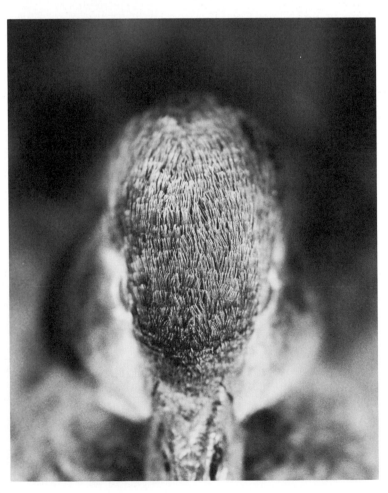

Head feathers. Note that very small feathers around forehead and front cheek area are visible. They look more like hairs than feathers and tend to swoop up above eyes and flow together down back of head.

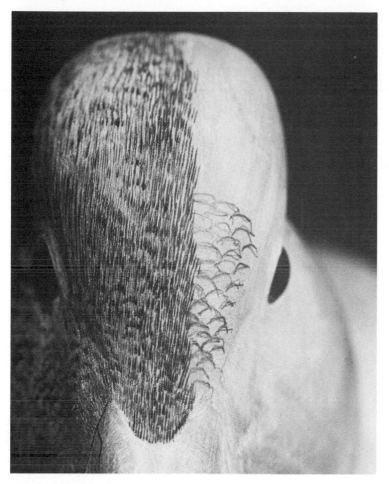

Head feathers laid out. Carve them very carefully with Xacto knife or grinder, cutting outline of each feather and then just sanding lightly. (They can also be outlined with pencil and woodburned in.)

Lay out primary feathers and cut out separately (with Xacto knife) from a sheet of basswood. You can cut one piece of wood and make four or five feathers from it or cut individual feathers. We use one piece or two at the most if we want to show feathers separated a little.

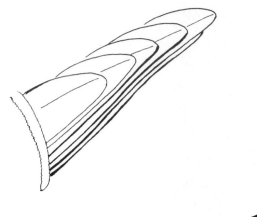

PRIMARY LAYOUT   How primary feathers stack. Note bottom feather is shorter.

Crossed primaries on redhead hen, showing short primaries.

Longer primaries on widgeon hen.

Once primaries are cut out, you can outline edge of each feather by relieving wood around edge with ruby carver. (File or knife may also be used).

Carving primaries with ruby carver. The edges on these feathers are the largest and thickest on the bird. Divers will have fewer primaries showing than do dabblers.

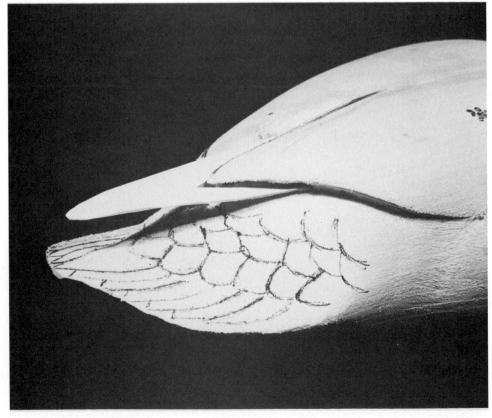

Primary group cut as one piece of wood being checked for length and proper fitting.

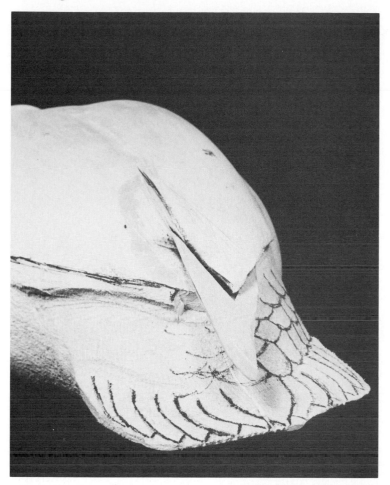

Primary group cut as one piece of wood being tested for length and fit. Some additional feather highlighting can be done by grinding certain areas such as side pockets. Several splits can be carved quickly with grinder.

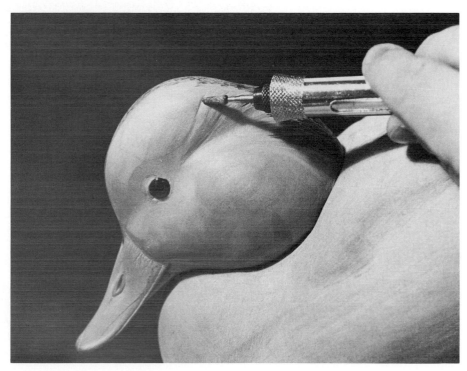

Accent marks or character lines can be ground into head area behind eyes. Experiment wherever you see lumps or bumps in the feathers. Once you grind areas you can go back and woodburn over the grinding, so be creative and have fun.

11

Woodburning and Texturing

By now you've had a chance to work with feather layout, feather carving, and other techniques in an effort to make your carving realistic. The next step is to add barbs, and at times quills, to the feathers on your carving. We accomplish this by either woodburning or stone texturing.

Many carvers rely solely on woodburning to achieve a controlled texture. Others recreate the free flow of feathers by stone texturing. A combination of the two techniques can produce excellent results. To give you a better insight, we'll describe both burning and texturing. You can decide which is best for you.

If you decide to burn, the first thing that you should acquire is a good burning pen such as the Hot Tool or Detail Master. The Hot Tool is a good choice for the beginning carver as it is a quality tool with available options, such as heat control and an array of changeable tips. Above all, it is low in cost.

To the more advanced carver, the Detail Master will definitely fill the bill. This advanced unit comes with its own central supply unit; it also has a variety of handpieces that can be changed in an instant. Of course, the price is reflective of the advanced features that it provides.

By practicing with your burning tool, you will acquire a feel as to how much heat to use to effectively carry out your burning. In fact, by varying degrees of heat, you can create light and dark areas for each feather, which is quite useful when carving birds, such as the mallard hen, that have brownish tones and patterns.

Avoid the habit of burning feather lines too deep (too much heat) and too far apart. Remember to keep your heat down and let the burning tip do the work for you. Don't force it! As long as you can burn a line without creating a lot of smoke, the heat should be sufficient. As with burning too deep, burning in the barb lines can also be a problem. Keep in mind that even a coarse feather has approximately fifty barbs to an inch, and sometimes even more. Burning is like any other technique used in carving: patience and practice are the keys to proficiency.

If you do not care to woodburn, you can use texturing stones and a power tool such as a flexible shaft machine. Although you can accomplish this type of texturing quite quickly, you will not have the control that you have when burning. This does not mean that you will not achieve the desired effect. It simply means that in burning, you can burn in a line close to another burned line with a degree of accuracy. With texturing, you have to acquire a feel for direction and depth of cut. If you're not satisfied with either technique, incorporate both burning and texturing in your carving and work out a happy medium.

Researching a feather will give you an understanding of quill size and the flow and density of the barbs.

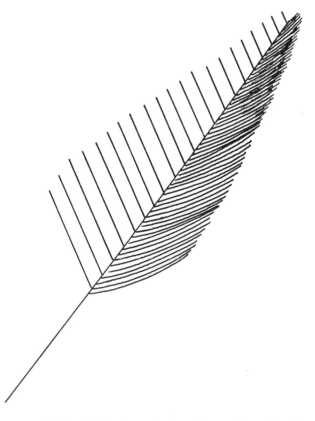

Don't get in the habit of creating straight quills and barbs. They curve and flow with the shape of the feather.

Feathers should not resemble evergreen trees. If they do, you are not taking time to do research.

Before burning or texturing, outline feathers in pencil. This will keep you aware of where feathers start and end.

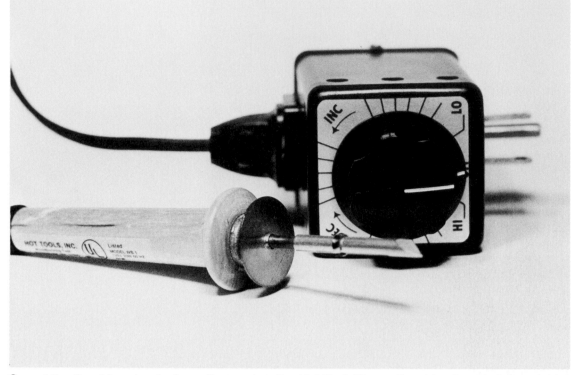

One of the finest burning tools on the market, the Hot Tool. The optional heat control rheostat is also pictured.

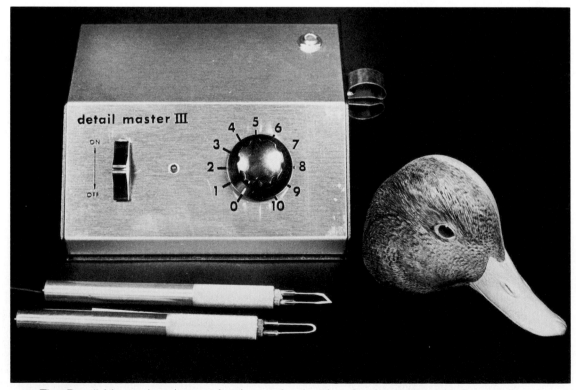

The Detail Master is a burner for the professional or for those who chiefly woodburn.

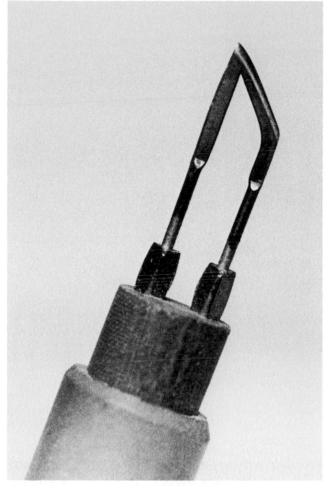

This is one of the burning tips we use most often, especially on the larger feathers. We also use this tip to burn in quills.

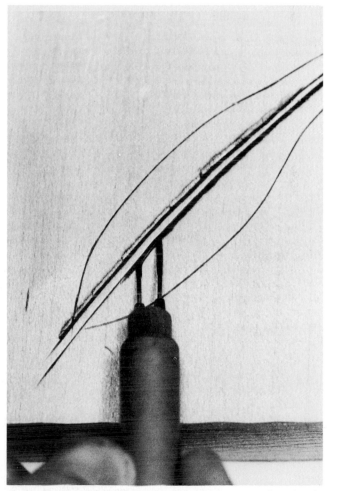

To burn in quills, first draw in the shape, then lay the tip on its side and burn down each side of the line.

After you've completed the burning, sand with medium to fine sandpaper so that quill is raised.

A burned feather should show continuity in the flow and shape of the quill and barbs.

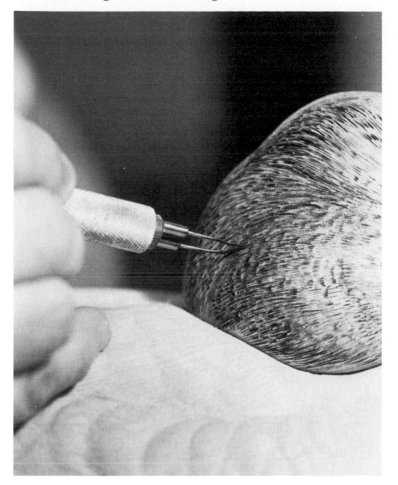

See photo (burning head)

Some of the finer feathers can be burned or textured without a noticeable quill.

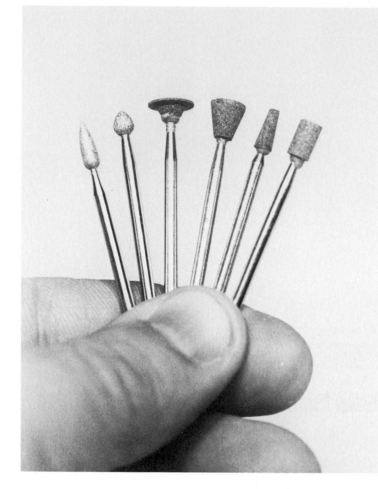

Some of the points that we use when texturing.

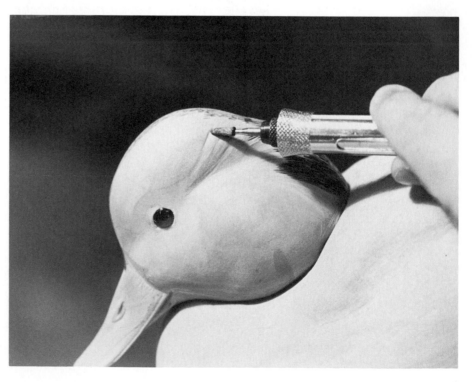

Indentations can be achieved and fine cuts can be made depending on the point used.

Splits in feathers can also be achieved.

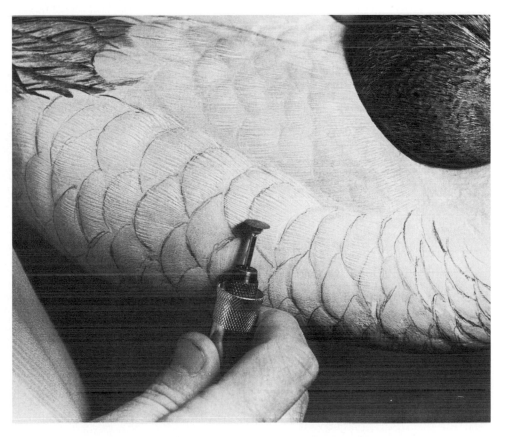

Finer lines can be created by using the edge of a disk shape.

After burning or texturing, brush out the textured lines (in the direction of the feather flow) with a toothbrush or motorized brush.

Tail feathers of a ruffed grouse. Burning has created the patterns shown.

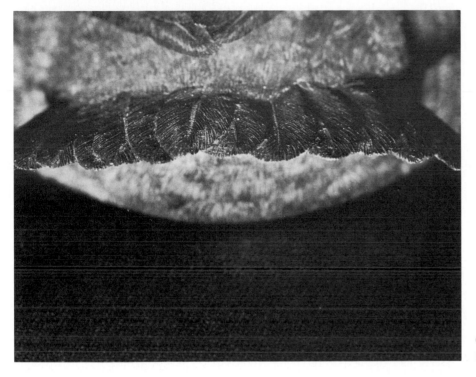

Close-up of redhead's tail wood-burned.

Burning can also be used under each feather to give it a raised look.

12

Hollowing the Body

There are two reasons for hollowing the body of a carving. The first, and most important, is to relieve pressure in the wood, which causes the wood to split. Hollowing greatly reduces splitting of the wood. The second is to make the wood lighter so the carving will float like a real bird. If you plan to enter your carving in a floating decorative class and the wood is heavy, consider hollowing. Chances are the carving will float too low in the water if you do not hollow the body.

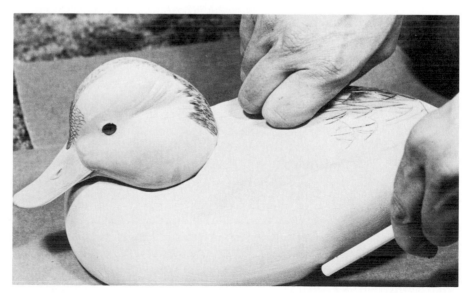

Place the bird on a piece of cardboard and trace around the body. Keep pencil point close to edge of body.

Remove bird and draw another line ½ inch inside first line.

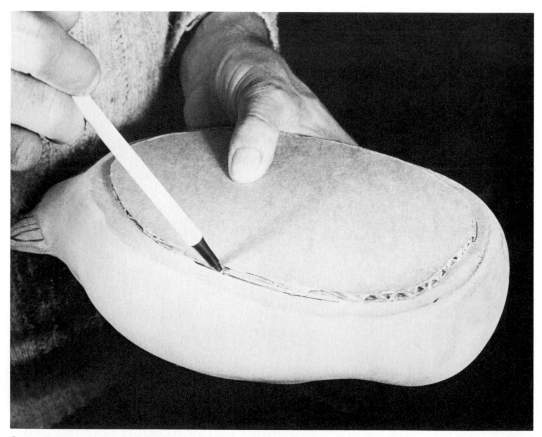

Cut out the small pattern (it should look exactly the same as the bottom of the decoy, only ½-inch narrower all the way around). Place oval-shaped cardboard on the bottom of the decoy and draw around cardboard on the block of wood. Save cardboard; it will be the pattern for cutting bottom plate later on.

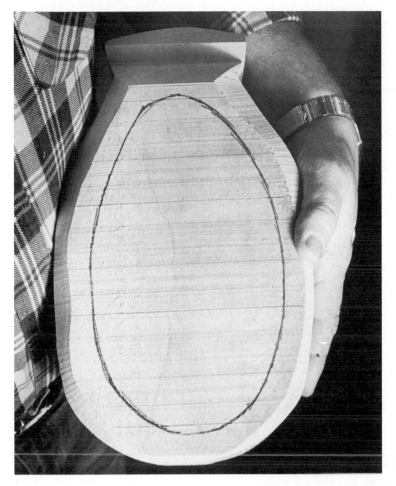

Bottom of decoy with bottom plate line drawn on.

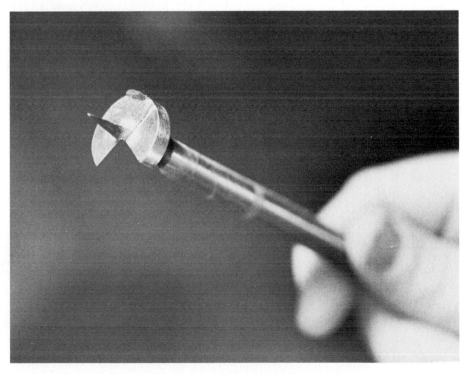

Use a Forstner bit in a hand drill or drill press to hollow the body. We use a Forstner bit ¾ or ⅝ inch in diameter. The point will come through the body if you slip, without leaving a large hole. It is easy to repair the small hole with wood filler.

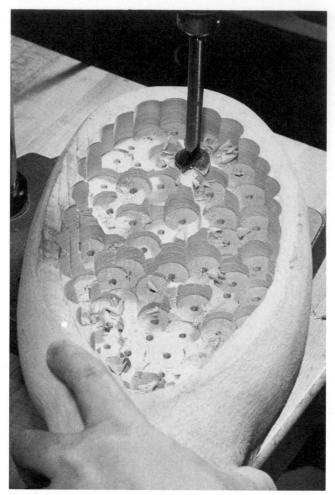

Place edge of drill on inside of line and drill about ¼ inch deep all the way around. Next, drill one half the width of drill head inside first row of holes. When you are done with the second row, you should have a ledge all the way around about ¼ inch wide. (This ledge is where bottom plate will rest before being glued down and screwed.) Now drill very carefully the rest of the body to a thickness of about 1 inch. Take extreme care not to drill through in low areas of the back.

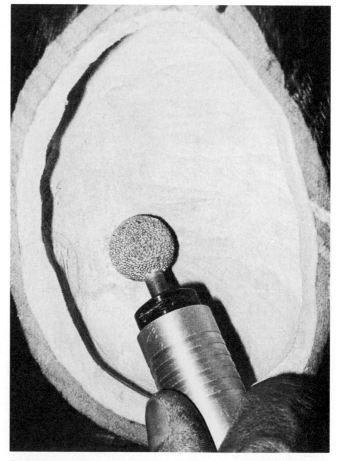

Once body is hollowed, use ball nose cutter to remove excess wood.

Body hollowed for bottom plate.

Now go back to your cardboard pattern and draw bottom plate.

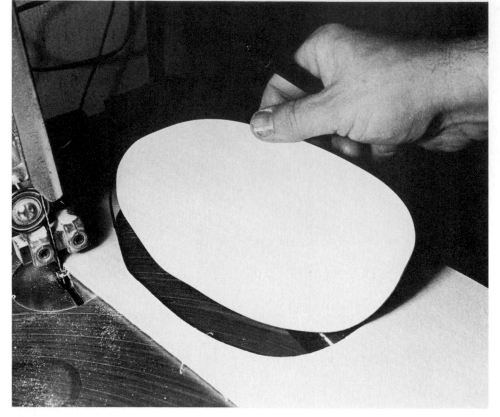

With a band saw, cut bottom plate about ¼ inch thick and fit it to the bottom by grinding or carving with a knife.

Bottom plate cut out and screw holes marked. (Note ledge to put plate on.) Before you screw or glue bottom plate on, wrap the bird in a cellophane bag and float it with bottom up. You will be able to see how the bird floats and can tape weights on inside of plate to balance it before sealing the bottom.

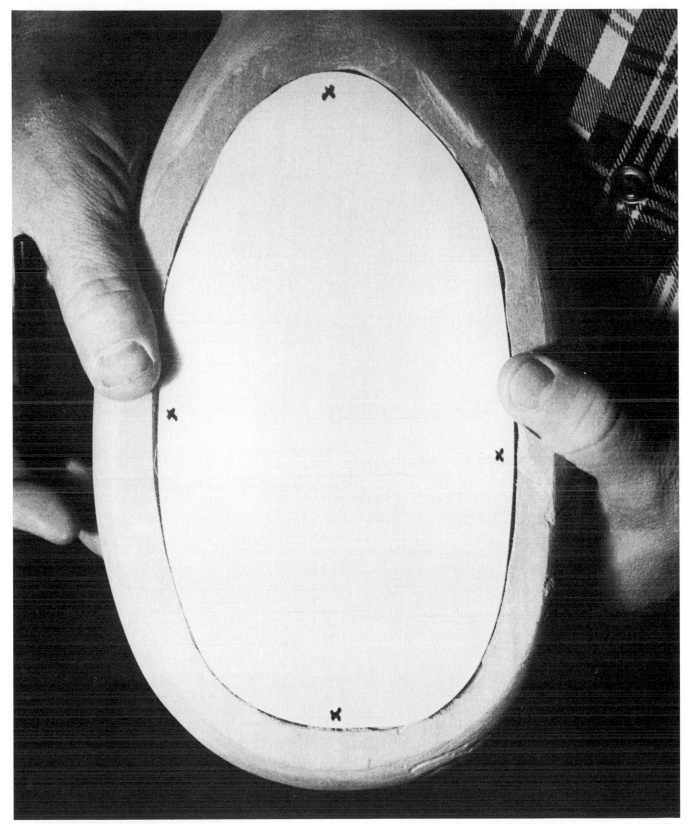

Bottom plate in place and glued down. Fill all the cracks that may be visible with waterproof wood filler and sand smooth. Seal bottom with paint, varnish, or any sealer to keep water out. Countersink and screw the plate on with brass screws (they don't rust).

13

Painting the Carving

When you've completed your carving to the best of your knowledge and ability, it is time for you to apply the coup de grace. In other words, it is time to add color to your creation.

Painting Supplies

Before we discuss painting techniques, we'd like to give you an idea of the supplies you'll need to prepare and paint your carving.

Sealers. It is important to seal your bird before painting so that the wood does not fuzz up and create a bumpy surface. The sealer we use is Deft Sanding Sealer and Krylon 1303 Acrylic Spray. Any other good-quality sanding sealer will do. If you use a sanding sealer, thin your first and second coats with

50 percent thinner so that it will be absorbed deep into the wood. Build it up so that you have a fairly hard surface, but make sure that you do not fill in your texturing or burn lines. We have found that four or five coats of sealer are sufficient.

Some carvers use a mild abrasive, such as fine steel wool or fine abrasive pads, between coats to eliminate small bumps. If you use an abrasive, take care not to rub out the fine detail you have strived and worked for. Make sure that you also brush away all residue from the steel wool or pad.

Gesso. Gesso is a chalky white painting base. It does the same job as primer does for the paint job on a car; that is, it gives the paint something to stick to. It also softens the colors so that the paint doesn't shine so much. Gesso is good for painting on carvings that do not have woodburning or texturing detail because, again, it gives the paint a solid, adhesive base.

Wood Bleach. If you're painting a bird that is light in color and you've completed the woodburning, you may have a hard time painting over the dark areas of the burn. Applying coats of Gesso will eliminate this. But you should be wary of filling in with Gesso if you are working in very fine detail. To lighten the wood, you can apply wood bleach. Carefully follow the directions on the bottle. Wood bleach can be obtained from your local hardware store.

Paints. It's up to you to decide which type of paint you would like to use, oils or acrylics. We prefer acrylics. Because they are fast-drying, acrylics enable you to blow-dry and add

An assortment of brushes, more than what is really needed.

successive washes. They are durable and the colors are stable. Blending acrylics, however, takes practice. Because of their fast drying time, you have to know what you are doing before you begin blending. Clean-up is easy, as is thinning. All you need is water.

Oils, on the other hand, take a long time to dry. To some people this means more blending time in which to create a realistic painting. Some top carvers still use and believe in oils. They are fully capable of doing the job. The long drying time is a big drawback, though, for most carvers. Clean-up and mixing are a little more tedious because of the need for thinners and special cleaners. If you do have a preference for oils, try the Alkyds. They're an oil-based paint, but the drying time is much shorter than that of ordinary oils.

Whichever medium you choose, we suggest you acquire a name brand such as Grumbacher or Liquitex. Stick with that one brand since names and colors may change with different brands. Also, while you're at it, acquire some small jars (baby food jars are excellent) or plastic containers. Use them to pre-mix and store colors so that you will not have to mix and match each time you paint. We have stored colors for up to four weeks in containers; by adding a drop or two of water or thinner, you can keep them even longer.

Brushes. One of the biggest fallacies in painting, be it flat work or decorative carvings, is that the brush is the answer to all of your painting problems. There is no denying that a good brush is an important asset, but it will not a painter make.

The choice of brush sizes is up to you. Some carvers use #000 brushes for the fine detail, whereas others use #1 or #2 brushes for the same work. Experiment! When selecting your first brushes, choose a #00 or #1, for detail; and ½-inch, 1-inch, and 2-inch brushes for painting washes and applying Gesso. As time goes by, you will probably acquire just about all the brushes on the market. Always remember to clean your brushes, and store them flat or standing with the bristles up.

Painting Palettes. When you start painting you will need something to mix your paint on. In our carving classes, we use rolls of white freezer wrap. It has a shiny side and a dull side. Use the shiny side; otherwise, the paint will saturate the paper. Freezer wrap can be cut to any width or length. You can also use wood, glass, or disposable palettes. This is your choice since they all do a good job.

Rags, Paper Toweling, and Water Containers. Keep these items on hand to clean and rinse your brushes during painting. Get in the habit of cleaning your brush periodically, even if you're using only one color. The brush will then be more receptive and perform better. If brushes are not cleaned, paint may start to thicken in the bristles and hamper performance.

Drying Unit. Any hand-held hair dryer will suffice. You do not need to burn off the paint when drying, so turn the fan up or set the dryer on medium. Of course, blow-drying is more applicable with acrylics, since they are water-based.

Alcohol. This is used to remove paint when you make a mistake. Put a small amount on a rag and rub, being careful not to eliminate any fine detail on the carving.

There are other supplies you can obtain to help you prepare and paint your carving; but as you will find out, you'll acquire timesavers and techniques as you progress. Remember, a right way and a wrong way is not always true. We might go with the adage, a right way and a *better* way. There isn't a carver or painter in the world today who has all the answers. So keep an open mind when you carve and paint. Who knows, you just might stumble onto something that nobody has ever done before.

Basic Color Theory

In order to paint with any degree of accuracy, the basics of color must be understood. To understand means study and practice are required. At times, color theory becomes very confusing, especially when you're given terms such as primary, secondary, tertiary, hue, shade, value intensity, and so on. All of these terms have meanings that we must know, but most of us want to paint without having to take a six-month course in color theory.

We all agree that there are many principles of color theory that do not apply to what concerns us, namely, painting decorative carvings. Let's also agree that the basics should be learned and put to use. We hope to give you a general understanding of what to expect from mixing different colors. If you're interested in becoming more knowledgeable about color theory, there are books to be read and courses to be taken at your local universities or schools.

The first principle to keep in mind is that there are three basic colors called *primaries:* red, yellow, and blue. (Fig. 1, page 129) From these three primaries all other colors, except white and black, can be achieved. In essence, this statement is correct if we use the correct primary colors, meaning a *true* red, *true* yellow, and *true* blue (not cadmium red, light yellow ochre, or thalo blue).

If we mix equal parts of primaries, we can produce more colors. Yellow and red create orange; red and blue create violet; yellow and blue create green. (Fig. 2, page 129) The colors created by the mixture of our primary colors are called *secondaries.* Knowing just this little bit about color combination can greatly improve your painting.

Many of the old masters used a glazing technique to add life to their paintings. A glaze is much like a wash, which lets each layer of color show through. For example, if a wash of red is applied over a base color of yellow, the light penetrates the layers, bounces off the yellow, and travels back through the wash of red, creating a vibrant orange. (Fig. 3, page 129) Remember? Our primary mix of red and yellow created orange. A technique like this is very useful when you are creating the iridescence of feathers—the play of light that produces the magnificent colors on a live bird.

Colors can perform tricks for you. Try layered washes on a sheet and see what you can create. Just remember to dry each wash before applying another one.

Now that you have experience in mixing primary colors to create secondary colors and have worked on washes, the color scheme can be carried a little further.

A new set of colors—*intermediate colors*—can be achieved by mixing primary and secondary colors. (Fig. 4, page 129) Since mixing an equal portion of primaries resulted in secondaries, the intermediate colors are created by adding more or less of a primary color to a secondary color. For example, mixing equal amounts of yellow and blue creates green. By adding more yellow to the mixture, we create yellow-green; by adding more blue, we create blue-green. The same holds true with the other colors: yellow and red mixed equally create orange; more yellow added creates yellow-orange; more red added creates red-orange. Add more blue to violet and you get blue-violet; more red creates red-violet.

With the three primary colors you have created nine new colors. Such experimentation can give you a good insight on what to expect from your paints. There is no magic way to learn everything about color, and many a good artist has learned simply through trial and error—and hard work.

Blending of Colors

Probably the biggest obstacle a beginning carver has to overcome when painting—especially with acrylics—is how to blend colors so that they look natural. Blending colors means that one color must flow smoothly into another with no sharp contrasting lines.

To perfect this technique takes practice. We use a practice technique that involves the shading of a circle so that it takes on the look of a ball. (Fig. 7, page 130) All that is needed is scrap paper (watercolor paper is a good choice) and paint. In the illustration we've used the colors Hooker's green, thalo blue, and cadmium yellow light on the green ball;

and cadmium red dark, cadmium red light, and cadmium yellow light on the orange ball.

Your first step is to determine where your light source is coming from and blend from this area all the way through to the darkest-shaded area. By practicing, you will acquire a feel for how much paint to add to darken or lighten. This is not an easy exercise. It takes a lot of practice, but eventually you will master the technique. Remember, the blend has to be smooth.

Painting

Once you've carried out all the necessary preparations in sealing your carving (see Painting Supplies, Sealers), you are ready to paint. Once again, if you would like to use Gesso, by all means do so. We have achieved excellent results by just painting over the wood color, after it has been sealed, of course.

If you do start with Gesso, tint it before it is applied. This means that you will study the areas to be painted—the head, back, side pockets, and so on. Determine the base color; it might be a dark brown, light brown, or in the case of the head, red or green. Once you have determined the base color, apply this color to your Gesso and mix it. Then apply (in thin coats) this mixture to each specific area. It is important that you thin your Gesso, with water, and build up each coat; otherwise, you run the risk of filling in your burning or texturing. Between each coat, blow-dry the area with a hand-held dryer.

Once you have acquired an even consistency of coatings, you can begin your actual painting.

A cardinal rule to follow is to apply all your paint in thin washes and blow-dry each wash before the next wash is applied. Questions keep arising on how thin or how thick a wash should be. If an acrylic wash is used, use water as a thinner. To explain washes: If you were to take a newspaper, mix a wash of a certain color and paint it over the newsprint, *and* the color shows, *and* you can still read the newsprint without any problem, then and only then do you have a wash of correct

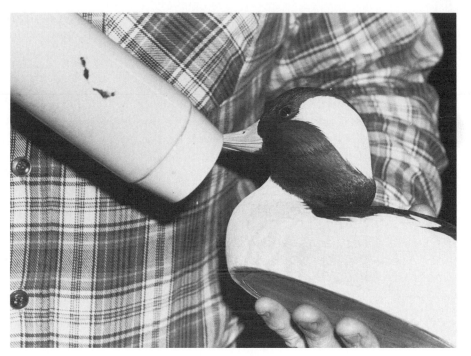

Blow-dry between washes until all traces of water disappear.

consistency. If your color is too faint, you are adding too much water. If you have a hard time reading the newsprint or you cannot see it at all, then you have a coat of paint appropriate for painting a house, not a decorative carving. (Fig. 8, page 130)

Take time to study our step-by-step painting of the heads of a woodduck drake and a mallard hen. (Figs. 9–12, pages 131–132) Even though they might seem limited in color, the procedure for painting these two species holds true for most others. It is just a matter of determining the correct colors for the species you've chosen.

Painting Iridescence

The first thing that we usually hear from a student when faced with the task of painting iridescence is, "How on earth am I going to reproduce *that*?" You might be asking, "What is iridescence?" Simply put, iridescence is the rainbow of colors produced by the play of light on the feathers of a waterfowl. It can be created to a certain degree with thin washes of paint.

To prove this point, we've illustrated the head of a drake bufflehead in various stages

of iridescence. (Figs. 15–18, pages 133–135) This is where your knowledge of blending colors (avoiding sharp contrasts between each color) is important.

In the carving world, there are supposedly magic elixirs such as iridescence paint and bronzing powders. They seem to perform a respectable job; but in the hands of a novice they can become a hindrance, creating a metallic, hard, or glossy look. Powders also seem to dull after a period of time. We believe that you can create just as much iridescence with your washes of paint as you can by using the gimmicks. You'll just need time and patience to perfect your technique.

Painting Vermiculation

What is vermiculation? Vermiculation is the wavy, dark bands or lines that are on the feathers of certain species of ducks.

Although it is tedious work, painting vermiculation is not all that difficult. All that is needed is a good pointed brush, either a #1 or #0, and paint thinned to the correct consistency.

When painting vermiculation, always paint the feathers first. In other words, create the highlights and shadows before vermiculation.

We should mention here that there are carvers who use an art or technical pen for the vermiculation. We are not condemning this procedure; but to us, painting is a much more fluid and controllable method. During painting, the intensity of color as well as the thickness of line can be varied more easily with a brush than with a pen. But if you try a pen and feel comfortable using it, by all means do so.

Patterns of vermiculation vary from one species to another. You will notice that some have a bold, intense pattern, whereas on others the pattern is very fine. This variation is caused by the feather itself. Since feathers are translucent, the lights or darks can be seen through them. If you have a mounted specimen, vermiculation, take the time to study the patterns.

As we mentioned earlier, you can create bold or fine, intense or light, vermiculation with a brush. (Figs. 17 and 18, pages 134–135) It is imperative that you add shadows and highlights to all of the feathers *before* you paint vermiculation.

Feathers of woodduck (left), redhead (center), and lesser scaup (right) show differences in boldness of vermiculation.

Painting Black

To most beginners, black seems like an easy color to paint. All you have to do is squeeze it from the tube and begin painting, right? Nothing could be further from the truth. In actuality, the blacks seen on various waterfowl have other colors showing also. If you have a study skin or mount handy, subject it to light and see what colors show up. You will be surprised. Some have a blue, green, or brownish cast, and others have more multiple colors.

This is why we use a mixture of ultramarine blue and burnt umber to create a black. Sometimes raw umber is used instead of burnt umber. Caution is required, though, since some manufacturers use more yellow in their mixtures, which can create a greenish mix.

When we mix a black by using the ultramarine blue and burnt umber, we are able to vary the amount of each color so that we can create a brown or blue-black. This black mixture also paints softer, which is the effect we are trying to achieve. There are times, however, when ivory and Mars black are invaluable.

When painting with this black mixture, create three values: dark, medium, and light. (Fig. 5, page 130) As black feathers also show shadows and highlights, you will be able to more realistically re-create feathers by using these three values. (Fig. 18, page 135)

Painting White

What holds true with black also holds true with white. It is perhaps one of the most difficult colors with which to attempt the softness required. The reason for this is the physical property of feathers. Since they are translucent, light passes through, creating softness, gloss, and depth. But when we paint opaque white over wood, we get a hard gloss with no depth or softness.

You should mix white so that you have, as with the color black, three values: dark, medium, and light. (Fig. 6, page 130) When we say dark, we do not mean black. You can vary the colors of your grays from a brownish gray to a bluish gray. Remember to create an illusion of shadow at the base of each feather. With this technique, the feathers have depth, not just an overall white appearance.

Try practicing on scrap paper. Paint the middle value first, add the dark value at the base, and the light value at the tips. (Fig. 18, page 135) Do not create sharp contrasts between each value. They have to blend into each other.

With the illusion of depth, you also get the impression of the feather's shape. One brush stroke will not achieve everything. Remember, we are working with washes.

Adding a touch of yellow ochre to the white will also soften intensity of the white, as sunlight also creates a yellowish cast. If your white becomes too yellow, you have added too much yellow ochre. Remember, things usually are not as they appear, and there are no solid black or white ducks.

It is foolish for us to believe that we will be able to re-create *all* the subtle tones and variations of each feather. We must always believe, however, that it is up to us, as artists, to create the *illusion* of feathers through our painting.

Painting the Bill

To many carvers, painting the bill falls into the all-black, all-yellow, or whatever color category. In other words, they do not take the time to study the variations of color. They see the bill as one color, and that's as far as it goes.

If you take the time to study these variations, you will be able to reproduce, with paint, a more natural look. Take, for instance, the bills of a mallard and a canvasback. (Fig. 19, page 135) Even though their colorings appear solid, areas such as the top of the bill, lip, and nostril, and the lower mandible are actually lighter and darker. Since you try to re-create highlights and shadows on the feathers, carry your efforts to the bill also. You will see an improvement in

the overall look of the bill area in your carving.

Your painting does not have to be as contrasting as we have illustrated (to make our point). Just create a subtle suggestion to emphasize these areas.

Color Schemes

To help you in your first painting projects, here are some lists of tube colors that we use to re-create the colors of several puddle and diving ducks.

Even though there are a multitude of species, color schemes are really not that different. For example, a base of green is applied for the coloration of heads on the drake woodduck, mallard, shoveler, and goldeneye. A canvasback, redhead, and green-winged teal all need a base of red. Even the hens have a common base color.

At first you may see such a variety of color and texture that you're completely bewildered. Remember, keep everything in context—search out the basic color and go from there. All the little things such as subtleties of iridescence and depth will come with experience.

We wish that we could prescribe a formula that would work for you with exact mixtures and ratios. Even though this sounds great, it is definitely not the way to learn. You must rely on your own initiative and persistence. Remember that old adage, *You learn by doing!*

When you look at the color lists for specific birds, please keep in mind that even though you have the colors necessary, it is up to you to achieve the desired effect. In fact, you will be better off acquiring a few painting boards and then practicing your blending and mixing before you touch the brush to your carving. Keep notes on the colors you use and what kinds of effects you achieve. It doesn't do any good to produce a desired result without knowing how you got there.

Painting is like discovering a new world, once you gain a little knowledge of the unknown. You'll be surprised by what you can do with your rainbow of colors.

Tube Colors to Use on Dabbling Ducks

Mallard Drake

Head	Hooker's green
	Thalo blue
	Thalo green
	Yellow
Bill	Cadmium yellow medium
	Raw sienna
	White
	Black
Breast	Burnt umber
	Burnt sienna
	Red ⎫ For a purplish wash
	Blue ⎭
Speculum (if showing)	Ultramarine blue
	White
	Thalo bluc
Cape	Burnt umber
	Touch of black
Tail	White
	Raw umber
Side pockets	White
	Black
	Raw umber or ultramarine blue to make a bluish or brownish gray
Back and Tertials	Burnt umber
	Black
	White
Rump	Ultramarine blue ⎫ Mix to black
	Burnt umber ⎭

Widgeon Drake

Head	White
	Raw sienna
	Raw umber
	Yellow ochre

Specks	Ultramarine blue Burnt umber	} Mix to black
Iridescent Patch	Thalo green Hooker's green Cadmium yellow light	
Bill	Cerulean blue Black White—to lighten mixture	} Mix to bluish gray
Breast	Burnt sienna Burnt umber Black White	
Body	Burnt sienna Burnt umber Raw sienna White	
Vermiculation	Ultramarine blue Burnt umber	} Mix to black and brownish black
Tail	Raw umber Raw sienna White Burnt umber	} Edge of feathers
Rump	Ultramarine blue Burnt umber	} Mix to black

Wood Duck Drake

Head	Hooker's green Thalo green Cadmium yellow light Napthol crimson Thalo blue White	} For iridescence and crimson around the eye
Bill	White Napthol crimson Black Cadmium yellow medium Cadmium yellow light	

Breast	Burnt umber Red oxide Thalo blue White Black
Side pockets	Yellow ochre Raw sienna White Black—for vermiculation
Back	Burnt umber } Mix to bluish black Ultramarine blue Thalo blue } Bluish wash on some feathers, Yellow } greenish on others
Tail and Rump	Ultramarine blue } Mix to black Burnt umber Thalo blue Napthol crimson } Use on flank Cadmium orange

Pintail Drake

Head	Burnt umber Raw sienna Raw umber Black
Bill	Cerulean blue } Mix Black White—to lighten mixture
Body	Ultramarine blue } Mix to gray Burnt umber White Raw umber Raw sienna—on some feather edges
Vermiculation	Ultramarine blue } Mix to black Burnt umber
Rump	Ultramarine blue } Mix to black Burnt umber
Tail	Raw umber White

Tube Colors to Use on Diving Ducks

Canvasback Drake

Head	Red oxide Red Yellow Mars black
Bill	Ultramarine blue ⎫ Burnt umber ⎬ Mix White—add to mix for highlights, don't paint directly with white.
Chest and Rump	Ultramarine blue ⎫ Burnt umber ⎬ Mix to black Mixture can also be used for vermiculation.
Back and Side Pockets	White ⎫ Ivory black ⎬ Mix to gray Raw umber or ultramarine blue—add a touch to make bluish or brownish gray. Mixture can also be used for bluish gray of tertials.
Tail	White Raw umber Black

Ruddy Duck Drake

Head, top of	Ultramarine blue ⎫ Burnt umber ⎬ Mix
Patch	White ⎫ Touch of yellow ochre ⎬ Mix to grayish white
Bill	Cerulean blue White Touch of black
Body	Red Cadmium orange Red oxide Yellow Burnt umber There are many variations that can be achieved with these colors.

Tail	Red oxide
	Burnt umber
	Touch of black

Ring-Necked Duck Drake

Head	Ultramarine blue
	Burnt umber
	Red ⎫
	Blue ⎭ Mix for purple iridescence

Bill	White
	Ivory black ⎫
	Cerulean blue ⎭ Blend to dark bluish gray

| *Ring on neck* | Burnt umber |
| | Burnt sienna |

Breast, Back, and Rump	Ultramarine blue
	Burnt umber
	Wash of thalo green in places on the back for iridescence.

| *Vermiculation* | Ultramarine blue |
| | Burnt umber |

Side Pockets	White ⎫
	Ivory black ⎭ Mix to gray
	Tint of raw umber or raw sienna
	(Observe upper feathers outlined in white.)

Tail	White
	Raw umber
	Black

Greater Scaup Drake

Head	Hooker's green
	Black
	Thalo green—use as iridescent wash
	Yellow
	(Head is dark, but when exposed to light has green iridescence.)

Bill	Cerulean blue
	White
	Touch of black—to darken and to use for nail

Breast and Rump	Ultramarine blue ⎫ Mix to black Burnt umber ⎭ Mixture can also be used for vermiculation.
Back and Side Pockets	White Ivory black (The base color should be darker.)
Tail	Raw umber Black White

Redhead Drake

Head	Red oxide Yellow Red Burnt umber
Bill	Cerulean blue ⎫ Black ⎬ Mix to bluish gray White ⎭
Breast and Rump	Ultramarine blue ⎫ Mix to black Burnt umber ⎭ Mixture can also be used for vermiculation.
Back and Side Pockets	White Ivory black Raw umber or ultramarine blue—add a touch to make bluish or brownish gray.
Tail	White Raw umber Black Colors can also be used for tertials.

Lesser Scaup Drake

Head	Ultramarine blue ⎫ Mix to black Burnt umber ⎭ Red ⎫ Mix for purple iridescent wash Blue ⎭

Bill	Cerulean blue White Touch of black—to darken bluish mixture and to use for nail
Breast and Rump	Ultramarine blue ⎱ Burnt umber ⎰ Mix to black
Back and Side Pockets	White Ivory black (The base color should be a little darker. Add touch of ultramarine blue or raw umber if bluish or brownish gray is desired.)
Tail	Raw umber Black White

Common Goldeneye Drake

Head	Hooker's green Yellow Black Thalo green
Bill	Ultramarine blue ⎱ Burnt umber ⎰ Mix to black White—for highlights
Back and Rump	Ultramarine blue ⎱ Burnt umber ⎰ Mix to black
Breast, Side Pockets, and White Patch	White Touch of yellow ochre (Remember that base coat should be a little darker.)

Putting It All Together

The painting of the drake lesser scaup (Fig. 20, page 135) is the type of illusion that we like to create on our decoys. Shadows and highlights are created on the bill, head, breast, and every other exposed area of the bird.

Creating a pleasing illusion is the mark of a good artist. Waterfowl have such beautiful colors, iridescence, and feather markings that it is a shame not to exploit them to some degree. This does not mean you should create gaudy, unnatural colors; rather, create suggestive, soft, complementary colors and markings that will show off your decorative carving in the same way they show off the real bird.

As we stated earlier, we wish that we could prescribe a surefire, easy way to learn how to paint. The only "magic" elixirs that we know of are patience, persistence, and a lot of hard work.

14

To Show or Not to Show

Now that you know how to carve and are all pumped up, set some goals for yourself. Will you carve for fun, profit, or to show? Whichever you choose, be proud of your work. If it makes you happy that is all that really matters.

If you choose to show your work you can start with local arts and crafts shows to bolster your ego gradually, or you can show with the best at any of the many quality shows across the country. Most shows have classes for the novice, amateur and professional carvers. Your first large show will be an eye-opener, to say the least. You will either be shocked by the fantastic quality and beauty of the carvings and learn from the experience, or wonder why you ever entered. We suggest you love every minute of it and learn from everyone around you. Above all, don't be embarrassed by your work; rather, look at it as a learning experience as we did. Chances are your carving will be every bit as good as our first entries were. We still have lots to learn and will admit it freely to any-

one. That's the reason we keep carving. We hope you will feel the same way.

We think you'll discover, as we did, that carvers are a great group of friendly, talented people; they're down-to-earth and willing to share their knowledge. This is evidenced by the growing number of seminars held around the United States and Canada. There are fees of course, but the teachers are worth every penny of the cost in most cases.

If you feel comfortable with your work, try entering the annual World Championships hosted by the Ward Foundation the last weekend in April. The show has been held in Ocean City, Maryland, where there is great seafood and atmosphere. Here you will meet and mingle with some of the best wildlife woodcarvers in the world. Their carvings are on exhibit for world recognition. They enter their work for their peers to judge, as you will. Remember, once you enter the contest you are at the mercy of your peers. So don't complain about the outcome; the judges are only human, capable of mistakes as we all

With more and more people entering the carving field, shows such as this should grow by leaps and bounds.

are. Accept your fate gracefully and with a positive attitude you will receive lots of help and improve greatly.

The judges at most large shows, such as the World Championships, the U.S. Nationals, or the North American Championships, are professional carvers. Some are also taxidermists, ornithologists, and game biologists. Judges are looking for several distinguishing features. Among them are a good likeness of the bird you have chosen to carve; how the bird floats if it is in a floating class; detail work on the feathers, feet, and bills; and an overall flow to the carving. If any part of the bird could be called critical, in terms of judging, it would be the head, which can impart immense feeling. Most important is your ability to achieve an animated look in your carving (a stiff carving with all the feathers in neat rows probably won't cause much excitement). We hope the techniques we've shared with you will help you create a realistic, lively work of art.

Shows in North America

California

Pacific Flyway Decoy Association
   Wildfowl Festival
P.O. Box 201
Arcata, CA 95521
June

Pacific Flyway Waterfowl Festival
P.O. Box 536
Quincy, CA 95971

Pacific Southwest Decoy Competition
731 Beach Avenue
Chula Vista, CA 92010
February

Iowa

International Decoy Contest
Affiliated Woodcarvers, Ltd.
P.O. Box 406
Davenport, IA 52801
Early August

Iowa Carving and Art Show
2815 W. Locust Street
Davenport, IA 52804

Louisiana

Louisiana Wildfowl Carvers &
   Collectors Guild
615 Baronne St., Suite 303
New Orleans, LA 70113
Early Fall

Maryland

Easton Waterfowl Festival
Tidewater Inn
Easton, MD 21601
Early November

Havre De Grace Decoy Festival
P.O. Box 339
Havre De Grace, MD 21078
May

Ward Foundation Wildfowl Arts Exhibition
P.O. Box 2613
Salisbury, MD 21801

Ward Foundation World Championships
P.O. Box 2613
Salisbury, MD 21801
Late April

Michigan

Michigan Hunting Decoy Contest and
   Great Lakes Floating Decorative Decoy
   Contest, Potters Lake, Davison, Michigan
c/o Larry Van Wert
2528 Rushbrook Drive
Flushing, MI 48433
Late August

North American Wildfowl
   Carving Championship
4510 Kircaldy Road
Bloomfield Hills, MI 48013
Late September

New Jersey

Cape May Waterfowl Carving Show
Convention Hall
Beach Drive
Cape May, NJ 08204
Mid-Summer

Clayton International Hunting
  Decoy Contest
Clayton Area
Clayton, NJ 08312
Mid-Summer

Somerset County Carving Wildlife Art Show
190 Lord Sterling Road
Basking Ridge, NJ 07920
Fall

New York

U.S. National (Oldest show in U.S.)
Great South Bay Waterfowlers Assn., Inc.
P.O. Box 36
Brightwaters, NY 11718
Late March

Ohio

National Nature Art Exhibition
3995 Horseshoe Bend Road
Troy, OH 45373

Ohio Decoy Collectors & Carvers Assn.
  (Working Decoy Show)
P.O. Box 29224
Parma, OH 44129
March

Pennsylvania

Academy of Natural Sciences
  "Wildfowl Expo"
19th and the Parkway
Philadelphia, PA 19130
Late November

Rotary Foundation of Media
World Class Woodcarving Show
12 Veterans Square
Media, PA 19063
Late June

York Carvers Contest
York College
Country Club Road
York, PA 17405
Fall

Virginia

Great James Bay River Decoy Competition
North Side Lions Club
c/o Fred Langshultz
1033 Cheswick Road
Richmond, VA 23229
Mid-February

Great Snow Goose Decoy Contest
Chinocoteague Island, VA 23336
Late Spring

Mid-Atlantic Waterfowl Festival
P.O. Box 651
Virginia Beach, VA 23451

Wisconsin

The Wausau Show
Birds in Art, The Leigh Yawkey
  Woodson Art Museum
12th and Franklin Streets
Wausau, WI 54401
September through October

Canada

Canadian National Exhibition
Toronto, Ontario
Canada MGK 3C3
Mid-March and late August